C000186804

Practical Classroom Management

Practical Classroom Management
A Guide for Secondary School Teachers

Mark Braine
Dave Kerry
Mike Pilling

David Fulton Publishers
London

David Fulton Publishers Ltd
2 Barbon Close, London WC1N 3JX

First published in Great Britain by
David Fulton Publishers, 1990

Note: The right of Mark Braine, Dave Kerry, and Mike Pilling to be identified as
the authors of this work has been asserted by them in accordance with the
Copyright, Designs and Patents Act 1988.

© Mark Braine, Dave Kerry, and Mike Pilling

British Library Cataloguing in Publication Data
Braine, Mark
    Practical Classroom Management: a guide for secondary school
    teachers.
    1. Secondary schools. Classrooms. Discipline
    I. Title   II. Kerry, Dave   III. Pilling, Mike
    373.11024

    ISBN 1-85346-137-7

All rights reserved. No part of this publication may be reproduced, stored in a
retrieval system or transmitted, in any form, or by any means, electronic,
mechanical, photocopying, or otherwise, without the prior permission of the
publishers.

Typeset by Chapterhouse, The Cloisters, Formby, L37 3PX
Printed in Great Britain by BPCC Wheatons Ltd Exeter

Contents

Introduction

This book is aimed at the trainee or probationary teacher who might value a compact, easy to carry handbook which would give all the practical advice for everyday classroom management.

The authors are all practising teachers in secondary education who have considerable experience in dealing with crisis management. As such we are convinced that much of this crisis management could be avoided altogether by an effective preventative approach. It is hoped that within the pages of this book might be found helpful practical advice, hints and tips of the kind that can only be readily absorbed when undergoing 'on the job training'.

In the authors' experience, many students and probationary teachers join a school staff, lacking an ability to respond quickly to crises in the classroom; such an ability is gained by experience over many years, often painfully. Many training institutions simply do not have the time, or in some cases lack staff with current classroom experience sufficient to instruct in basic classroom procedure. Often this area becomes neglected in favour of academically credible work and the students are left to find out for themselves.

The James Report of the 1970's was overtaken by events. This advocated greater devolution of teacher training in schools, and allowed for a system employing mentors or tutors based there. Each student would be attached to such a tutor. However, the shelving of this report was caused in part by the massive reorganisation of teacher training due to falling rolls in schools. Recent events suggest that a more successful recruitment of teachers in shortage subjects may be brought about by substantially changing the nature of training offered to them: making it school, rather than college based. Whilst this may be politically motivated and indeed be opposed by various educational pressure groups, there is no doubt that the trend is once more towards increasing training within schools rather than the current 'short burst' teaching practice approach. Whatever the outcome, there is a perceived need for a handy sized reference book, which whilst not providing all the answers, is capable of suggesting possible avenues of approach for the novice teacher.

The basic tenet of this book is that good classroom management will have a preventative function and stop problems arising with behaviour; that much poor behaviour both in and out of the classroom can be diminished or even prevented by thinking ahead; that by following a set procedure, trouble can be avoided; and, finally that teaching is potentially a pleasurable, worthwhile and rewarding way of earning a living even during a period of great upheaval and uncertainty.

In writing this book, we have borne in mind the fact that many people will wish to 'dip into it' rather than to read it from beginning to end, and the chapter headings have been designed to facilitate this. Crucial to the modification and control of behaviour are considerations such as the social mix of various pupils, lighting and the layout of furniture appropriate to the type of lesson being taught. For example, can every pupil see and hear the teacher? All these aspects are covered by using exercises, simulations, examples and anecdotes.

Many teachers of considerable experience are still unaware of the procedures for referral outside school. These are usually learnt when a teacher accepts a promotion to a post of pastoral responsibility. The role of the Schools Psychological Service, that of the Education Welfare Service, the importance of community policing and the scope of home/school liaison are all areas which should be understood broadly during the early years of teaching. We share the view that ALL teachers have a pastoral responsibility and these are matters of which all should be aware: hence a chapter outlining these areas is included.

All teachers are concerned with allowing their pupils to reach their fullest potential, but in practice how does the inexperienced teacher bring this about? We examine practical ways of helping pupils by means of identifying and understanding needs and preparing appropriate materials, whilst a further chapter gives suggestions in tackling 'undesirable' behavioural traits. Other practical aspects of a teacher's day to day job which are covered include report writing, marking work and record keeping (now a contractual obligation) whilst a check list of 'do's and don'ts' has also been included.

It is our earnest hope that this book fulfils the function of providing a ready made source of advice and information of the type which is difficult to gain except by being employed in a school for a long time. It will give the new entrant into the profession greater security by stripping away the mystique attached to the craft of our job. The skills involved in teaching (rather that 'education' in its broadest sense) are those that are passed on from generation to generation, usually by example or word of mouth. If this book has contributed to the process, we shall have achieved our object.

Finally we would like to record our thanks to Jane White for typing the manuscript.

Mark Braine, Mike Pilling, Dave Kerry
June 1990

CHAPTER 1

Physical Aspects of Classroom Organisation

Many of the factors which influence pupil behaviour are outside your control; others are not. It is important to be able to differentiate between them; to accept that some aspects require you to build your procedures around them, whilst others you will be able to recreate in such a way as to provide the ethos of learning and progress of the type you desire. Developing this point further: these unmovable factors will dictate the content and style of the delivered curriculum, by the level of your target setting for pupils and your expectation of them. Let us look at these in more detail. They are:

- composition of catchment
- resources, equipment and fittings in the school
- the physical environment of your classroom
- the groups to which you are assigned
- the curricular dimension

Location of the school

The variety of school location is almost infinite, ranging from the 150-plus pupil secondary school in a county with scattered rural communications, such as Lincolnshire, for example, to a large urban comprehensive with 1,000 pupils. The atmosphere of a school can be dictated by this factor quite strongly: for example, if a school is located in a deprived urban community with a high level of unemployment, the opportunities for work experience programmes may be limited; there may be a perceivable requirement for physical barriers between this school and its surrounding areas, high fences, reinforced glass in windows and a 'fortress' attitude. It must be said, however, that there are many inner city schools which have developed excellent community links and are sound examples of good home-school liaison practice. The essence of the argument is that the location will *influence* thinking in the school. Equally, an area which suffers high unemployment may be better placed to call upon voluntary help by parents during working hours; examples could be the areas of self-help building and alteration schemes or in classroom support. The presence of a busy main road adjacent to the school could influence the curriculum by the placement of road safety aspects, whilst proximity to local firms might bring about links from which sponsorship schemes, 'compact' agreements and work experience programmes might arise.

The location of a school will also dictate the composition of the staff. In a rural area, it is likely that your colleagues will travel some distance to work, often being based in towns some miles away. Out of school activities, clubs and sports teams will be influenced by this, as will in turn the level of commitment by pupils, their sustained interest in their school and, ultimately, their behaviour.

These are factors about which, as a new classroom teacher, you can do little, but your analysis of your classes using this background information will help towards understanding of your pupils. If a child has a long rural bus ride home at the end of a school day, or has the responsibility of looking after younger brothers or sisters (for parents who both work) in a busy urban area, these factors will influence how you deal with her. The setting of homework, the detaining of pupils after school, your approach towards lassitude or tiredness exhibited by individual pupils in the classroom will be responses that you will be required to make to a 'fixed' situation.

Composition of the catchment

Historically speaking, the revolution in education is almost complete; we are moving to a situation in which the pace of change is accelerating but one in which the pupil make-up of the school might not be so constantly related to a geographical area; in this model parents eschew their neighbourhood schools in favour of those with a 'popular' image, those which obtain a large number of high grade examination passes or radiate some other form of attraction. In the latter category are the City Technology Colleges (C.T.C.s) appearing in the 1990s as a result of the 1988 Education Act. These no longer relate to a geographical catchment area but draw pupils from across the city in which they are situated. Since parents have to apply to such schools and there is a ceiling on their numbers, they are selective in essence, and in this way are more closely related to the grammar school ethos than that of the comprehensive.

If the school in which you teach is within travelling distance of a C.T.C., it is likely that the composition of the groups that you teach will be affected by transfers to the C.T.C.

Therefore, whilst your school may draw from the geographical area previously assigned as its 'catchment' area, other factors will be at work. Your school may be in an older urban area but, by virtue of examination results attract pupils from areas with a different social mix. Alternatively, your school may not enjoy a high level of parental support, with poor attendances at parents' consultation evenings, little support for extra curricular activities or a fundamental disagreement upon the social and education aims of the school. Such factors may have a historical dimension, and, despite your own approach in the classroom arising from a positive wish to overcome these difficulties, the background against which you work is largely outside your control.

The secret is to be *aware* of such factors and adapt your approach accordingly, remembering that, in such cases, the opportunities which you create for your classes, however, grudgingly received (or rejected) will represent a route along which your charges may develop giving them greater future social mobility.

It is vital that you take such information into account: you must allow pupils to draw from their own experiences and offer material to them to which they can relate. This does not mean a poverty of material, but attempting to engage your pupils' interest in, for example, a type of English literature with which they have had little contact, would be courting disaster. Your aim is to broaden their experience, but you must find common ground first.

To continue with our example of English literature: by emphasising that the human condition is universal, it will be possible to relate the way in which pupils might behave in their own familiar situation to that which occurs in a novel, play or poem. Such is normal good teaching practice, but, by allowing pupils to explore a dimension with which they are not familiar by means of those factors which are, you are demonstrating that you are aware of the social origins of your class.

Resources, equipment and fittings in the school

Your classroom approach, planning and preparation of lessons, plus, ultimately, your control, will be subtly influenced by the amount and quality of physical equipment available for your use in school. Whatever your subject specialism, such equipment will be fundamental to your style. On a simple level, it is always good practice to have available your own supply of pens and other simple equipment. Carry these in a box or in a tray to overcome the organisational difficulties and challenges created by pupils who avoid providing their own. This ensures a smooth and relaxed start to a lesson, avoiding the inevitable disruption and disturbances created by the hunt for suitable equipment.

The availability of computers and word processors is another area of effect: as schools move away from the rigid compartmentalisation of information technology and the use of separate computer suites, the number of computers in your department and their availability to you will affect the composition of your lessons. A child who may be potentially disruptive due to poor technical skills in the area of written expression may be perfectly confident in the use of a keyboard. Such a pupil may therefore be allowed to produce a proportion of his written work in this way: the availability or otherwise of a computer for use by the pupil either in or near your classroom becomes critical to the maintenance of his interest, and thus the smooth progression of your lesson.

The use of video or film equipment is, of course, dependent upon your ability to operate it in a 'readyuse' condition. Does your school have a resources technician who is available to you for setting up such equipment? Of course, you may be competent to do so yourself but in all likelihood will not have the time. The choice of a particular novel or play for use by your class may well be influenced by the credibility of a video tape which will enable you to bring the work alive for your group. Thus your preparation for a scheme of work is fundamentally affected by technical equipment.

Structural facilities, such as a gymnasium, playing field, drama studio or stage will all have a bearing on your classroom presentation, assuming that the school timetable will allow their use at a time when you are teaching the relevant subject.

The physical environment of your classroom

Never be afraid to use the shape and layout of your teaching area creatively. By this we mean that you should always be aware of your room's potential; it is quite likely that it will be a utilitarian 'box' filled with furniture which may, or may not, match. It is quite common to have to teach a fifth year group seated at desks or tables which they are 'wearing' on their knees! Chairs and tables often do not go together, breakages and their subsequent replacements causing a wide variety of mismatching. This is more relevant than at first it might appear, as long periods of still concentration can be difficult even for the most motivated pupil who is having to endure an insecure and uncomfortable wooden chair; lack of attention or fidgeting is understandable in such circumstances.

Again, be aware of your groups as individuals; take into account different ages with regard to furniture organisation and the planning of the various segments of your lesson plan.

Each group you teach will exhibit a different 'chemistry' or mix, depending on age, gender mix, ability range and other factors. Do not feel obliged to maintain the same seating plan for every type of lesson. Much will depend upon whether the room you are using is the one regularly assigned to you, or whether a sharing or pooling arrangement exists within a department, or indeed if you are substituting for an absent colleague in a room with which you are not familiar.

Let us develop this point further. An average room will be filled with up to thirty-five desks and chairs together with (usually, but not always) a teacher's desk and chair. It will feature a chalkboard or melamien-type writing surface, perhaps lockers or cupboards and at least one, but more likely several, power points. The room may have a blackout facility for film or video use, in which case you may find that you are having to exchange rooms from time to time with colleagues who lack such a facility. Additionally if you are in a room in a building dating from the mid 1950s to the late 1970s, it will feature large areas of glass, and is likely to possess a half glazed door from the external corridor. This last feature is of more note than you might imagine: as a new teacher you will be very aware and perhaps nervous of visitors to your classroom. It is also a perfectly natural tendency to be aware of movement in the corridor, creating a gravitational movement of you, the teacher away from the door sightline. This will affect your teaching position and stance.

Similarly, if you plan a lesson in which there is an element of class instruction and boardwork, the seating will need to be arranged so that all pupils can see the chalkboard. Indeed, the room is likely to be arranged in this fashion when you inherit it – and, as we will observe at other points in this book, there is nothing inherently wrong with such a traditional layout *when the circumstances demand*. However, it may be felt that with groupwork or individual study, this is inappropriate. Certainly there is an inherent level of formality in a seating plan featuring rows of desks and chairs facing the chalkboard. Another approach is to arrange the tables in such a manner so as to allow groups of four, five or six pupils to be seated around a 'block' of tables. This is a common arrangement. It has the advantage of allowing pupils to spread work out and pool resources; it also allows group oral work, now mandatory in many subjects, the reading of plays and graphical or art work also. The greatest disadvantage to you might lie in the less formal atmosphere and the consequent temptation for pupils to gossip and lose attention; additionally, you may find that some pupils will have their backs turned towards you, which may not be appropriate to the teaching style that you wish to adopt. This could be overcome by avoiding standing in one place, moving constantly around the room – which is good practice anyway. Try not to adopt the habit of remaining seated at a desk yourself; this makes your observation and thus your control static, and allows pupils not directly in your line of sight to misbehave. In fact by your body language you are transmitting messages to your group – as a mobile teacher, alert and aware, you are communicating your interest in and your obvious supervision of your pupils simultaneously.

In some lessons, you may wish to dispense with desks and tables altogether; do not feel reticent about this – clear the furniture against one wall if you wish to add a drama ingredient or to create simulation exercises illustrating whatever activity or theme you are pursuing. In a discussion, oral or group reading session you should feel free to dispense with desks: make a circle or semi-circle of chairs with you as a part of the circle. Again, this transmits a message: you are more obviously involved in the activity yourself, contributing on a more equal basis with the pupils: your control is still evident, but it has a more subtle dimension.

Again, memorise the position of power points for the use of electrical or audio-visual equipment; additionally, it is quite likely that the school will have at least one extension lead somewhere on the premises if your room is poorly supplied with points.

If the room is a technology workshop or laboratory, the 'fixed' element is more dominant. Science benches cannot be moved; nor can workshop equipment. However you can obtain a more fluid approach here, too. The 'led' or whole class teaching lesson develops into individual approaches in the same way, and the pupils will group according to the activity you set them. If, for example, the group is working on a technology project which requires multi-disciplinary design work in different materials, it is quite likely that individuals or groups will be moving freely around a technology area, with the fixed equipment being variously used by individuals at different stages in their developmental work. Similarly, groupings in a science laboratory will depend on the amount and the distribution of available equipment. For example, in an experiment requiring the use of heat applied by a bunsen burner, the number of such burners available will dictate group numbers and the deployment of your pupils around the laboratory. Equally, the number of textbooks will exercise influence on group numbers.

It may be that you have several different tasks that you wish followed during a 'practical' lesson, or a range from which pupils may choose; this is a strategy used with a group of mixed-ability pupils. The same may apply to any type of practical lesson.

With physical education the dynamics of the activities produce a different set of organisational challenges. Here, once more, the provision of fixed equipment in a gymnasium determines a certain amount of structure – wall bars and climbing ropes, for example. However the same strategies apply, according to the method of teaching you wish to adopt during that lesson. The pupils may sit semiformally on the floor in a circle or semi-circle whilst you give an explanation of what is required. They then move to the planned activity, which may be single or multiple, depending upon the number of staff and pupils involved.

In all practical situations, the notion of the safety of your pupils is paramount (as indeed it is at any time when you are *in loco parentis*) although where pupils are moving about, and there is the danger of accident, it is more pressingly crucial. This will dictate your organisation. Regulations such as pupil/teacher ratios and safety rules (which sometimes vary with local education authorities) are also influential.

In one sense, your teaching space is just another facet of the equation which you adopt to achieve your aim – the progress and development of your pupils. It may be summarised thus:

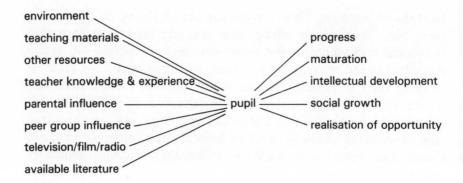

environment
teaching materials
other resources
teacher knowledge & experience
parental influence ———————— pupil
peer group influence
television/film/radio
available literature

progress
maturation
intellectual development
social growth
realisation of opportunity

However, we would suggest that environment (which for the purposes of this chapter, encompasses your teaching area) is a significant part of pupil development and learning experience. Therefore we would urge you to be creative and flexible in your approach to the use of this space. All the approaches discussed here are of equal validity and can be used as appropriate to the type of lesson that you wish to run.

We would, however, issue a note of caution at this stage, part of a theme developed throughout this book – and it is this:

(1) adopt styles with which you feel at ease rather than those of education fashion, since your relaxation will make you a more effective communicator and thus enhance the quality of your control.

(2) ensure that your pupils know exactly what you require of them at all times.

Whilst this might encompass clear instructions as to specific tasks, in the matter of classroom management this requires clear parameters within which to work. Applied to the matter of seating, it may well be advisable to adopt a more formal approach to start with; seating your pupils in formal rows until you know their names is to be recommended. Being able to address each individual by name is a key ingredient in classroom control, and it is to court disaster to have pupils working in groups before you know who they are.

It is quite common to have difficulty recalling names in the first few weeks of taking over new classes; particularly in your first year at a new school, where *all* pupils will be new to you.

A simple approach to this is to create a seating plan for each class; ask each pupil to introduce him or herself on the first day after having invited them to find a seat. Explain clearly that you would like them to always occupy that seat in your lessons, taking careful note of any undesirable combinations. You may wish to move these, or to take the risk and allow free choice of seating position. Make it clear that you reserve the right to move people later if the arrangement proves unsatisfactory. It may well represent a compromise by allowing such potentially troublesome liaisons to occur in order to learn names quickly, but if your retentive memory needs such help it will prove worthwhile.

Having made your plan, paste it into your mark book, diary or any other suitable place amongst the equipment you take to every lesson. It is then available for you to glance at before addressing any pupil, by name, in a confident manner! You may care to make it obvious to your pupils that this is what you are doing – once established it will become commonplace and unworthy of comment. By this time you will be largely familiar with your charges. Once you have reached this stage you will feel confident to vary the seating. Of course it is perfectly possible to adopt this strategy using *any* seating plan providing that it is consistent. In our view, however, the formal approach leading to a later relaxation is preferable.

The groups to which you are assigned

A further physical dimension is that created by the groups that you teach: their size, composition and group interaction. The physical influences referred to in the preceding section are dictated by the structure and fittings of the room in which you are teaching. The structure of your groups will likewise be influenced by physical limitations – your seating plan will depend upon numbers, gender mix and other considerations also.

We have already referred to the necessity of knowing the identity of your pupils at an early stage in order to exert your will where appropriate, and to set procedures and goals which are in accord with your philosophical aims. The next stage is to glean as much information about behavioural traits, background information and academic ability as possible. Do this as soon as is practicable so that you may organise balanced sub groups within the class other than those dictated by self-driven social groupings.

You will quickly find that certain members of the group will display unwanted behaviours and, in extreme cases challenging behaviours. The aim should always be preventative in these cases. One of the most effective ways of dealing with this is to identify such behaviours at an early stage; such an identification precedes a sorting process in which combinations of individual behaviours considered to be disruptive or undermining of your authority are eliminated. Awareness of this will allow you to take remedial action if you deem it necessary at a later date.

Let us assume that you have identified that one of your class is deaf or has a vision defect. Your strategy for dealing with this would be relatively straightforward in that you would arrange for this pupil to sit where his disability would not stunt his progress. By doing this you may then rearrange the social groupings which you allowed to form naturally, as described earlier. A less obvious difficulty may be presented by pupils who exhibit traits which slow down their progress. Take, for example, the case of the pupil who although pleasant and cooperative, is dreamy and lacks concentration. Clearly it would not be feasible to seat that pupil near to anyone who is creating disturbances or distractions.

Your movement strategies around the classroom will take cases like this into account; such a pupil will respond to frequent 'over the shoulder' checking and encouragement, therefore you are likely to closely monitor progress.

Other pupils in your groups will lack the necessary equipment such as pens: we have already stressed the desirability of having spare pens and other equipment with you to discourage time wasters, although it is important to retain a sense of balance and not to allow pupils to become dependant upon you for supplies.

You may also become aware of pupils who:

- fail to follow instructions
- fidget
- always finish first
- are orally confident but weak in written work
- ask for extra homework
- express a need to visit the toilet often
- always want to sit near the teacher
- laugh and giggle inappropriately

There are of course many behaviours, both desirable and otherwise that you will encounter in your classes. The important facts to remember are that

- all your charges are individuals upon whom your personality and behaviour will have a profound effect, and

● that you will need a range of strategies to deal with the range of behaviours that you will encounter. We will explore some of these strategies in later chapters.

The curricular dimension

As already discussed, the subject area in which you will be working will have a profound effect upon the physical opportunities and limitations of your teaching space. There will be other influences at work on your relationships with your classes, largely outside your control. When you first take over a new group, you will inherit the effects of these influences, and how you deal with them will be crucial to your control. Such influences can be summarised as follows:

(1) the regard in which your subject is held by the pupils
(2) the relationship between your predecessor and your groups
(3) (of an exam group) previous examination results in your subject
(4) the timing of the lessons, i.e. their placement in the school day
(5) the perceived 'strength' of the department in which you work
     – by the school management
     – the parents
     – the LEA inspectors
     – the pupils themselves
(6) the curriculum that you will be required to follow

All these factors form a backcloth against which you will be required to work; some will have a beneficial effect upon your teaching, others less so. However, none of them will necessarily undermine your control, and as your relationship with your groups develops, influences originating outside your classroom will be secondary to how your pupils view *you* – but it is important that you are aware that such dimensions exist within a school.

Your subject

Various messages are given out in any school and in some there exists a 'hidden hierarchy' of subjects. This may exist for historical reasons – for example a weak or disorganised Head of Department could have allowed the internal organisation of the area to deteriorate with a loss of morale, efficiency or application. Alternatively, at some stage the school management may have transmitted a message to the school either consciously or unconsciously by the way in which your subject is funded – the amount of school capitation allotted to it, or the amount of time it is granted on the timetable or, indeed the level at which it is staffed.

The relationship between your predecessor and your classes

Certain habits and work practices will already be in place when you take over a group as a result of the pattern of procedures laid down by whoever taught them before. It may well be that certain pupils have been given responsibilities within the class and will be expecting to maintain the status that this has afforded them. Pupils may sit in a particular order of placement or your predecessor's teaching styles may be in direct contrast to your own. The class may be used to didactic teaching or groupwork; the standards of discipline and behaviour may be at variance with those you wish to maintain. In these cases it is vital that you stamp your authority on the group as soon as possible. Do not, however, be tempted to overreact to the situation. Calmly explain to the groups how you wish to work and above all else be consistent in how you proceed. If you say you are going to act in a particular manner, always do so – set targets and parameters from your first day onwards.

Exam performance

There will be a history of exam performance in your subject area, perceived by the school management, the pupils and, most importantly, by the parents. If large numbers of pupils have not been entered in previous years, or have failed to achieve anything other than the basic GCSE grades, or have failed to gain many grades in the A–C range, your subject will be perceived to have a certain status or quality, both in comparison to other areas of the school and against a national or regional trend. The advent of the National Curriculum and published test results will not diminish this syndrome.

It is also possible that your subject area does not offer public examination opportunities; this is quite possible in such areas as Physical Education, Personal and Social Education and other subjects. Of course, in many schools this is not the case, but there is a tendency by parents to dismiss those subjects which do not yield an exam result. Such attitudes may not necessarily be reflected by the pupils however, and many are more open minded than their parents! Under these circumstances, it pays to avoid preconceived notions yourself and to play down any such sentiments expressed in your classes.

Timing

A pattern of behaviour will quickly emerge which can be linked with the timetable slot your lessons occupy. For example, if you meet a group during the last period of the day, three days a week, one of them Friday, your pupils are less likely to be alert and motivated before you even see them. Additionally, a little detective work will reveal the subject timetabled immediately before yours; an active outdoor lesson a few minutes previously will lead to widely different behavioural patterns from one in which the pupils have worked in strictly maintained silence. By consideration of these aspects you will be able to plan your lessons accordingly. For example, it would be more efficient to expect a group to concentrate hard on an extended piece of writing early on Monday morning when they are generally alert, not too hungry and have not already been exposed to long periods of concentration, rather than at the end of a busy week. During one of your lessons boisterous behaviour may be more apparent than on the other occasions when you see them: ensure that the work that you plan for that lesson allows for this.

Perceived strength of the department

The department in which you work will be a team, or at least that will have been a stated aim and a well run example will be supportive to you in your work. Pupils are extremely perceptive and are usually aware of departmental hierarchies. It is usual for departmental policy to have evolved various strategies, attitudes and procedures which will be standardised. These may, or may not, coincide with those espoused in other areas, although, they will usually fit within the federal framework of the school. However, pupils often associate a particular suite of rooms with a pattern behaviour or a level of expectation placed upon them by staff. You will be expected to operate within this scenario, but knowledge of how your immediate colleagues work will enable you to be aware of how the pupils perceive the way that they are expected to behave or work. During your probationary or induction period, it is quite likely that you will be offered the opportunity to observe how your colleagues operate; if this is not built into your induction period, ask for it to be made so – such observation will provide you with essential background information.

Parents' consultation evenings provide another dimension, clues to which will be littered through your conversations with parents over their child's individual progress. Their expressed concerns may imply a reputation which the department or faculty has gained, especially if reiterated by several parents individually. Be alert for hidden messages.

The level of support afforded by L.E.A. advisers or inspectors is another indicator. Indeed, discussions with advisers may contain frank comment, but it is usually apparent if the department in which you are working is regarded as an example of good practice. If there is a tendency to the opposite viewpoint it may manifest itself in frequent visits, written reports or even full inspections.

Again, the point must be made that many of these factors are outside your control; however do not assume that you are incapable of influencing them in the long term. One efficient and well regarded teacher working within a mediocre organisation can do much to enhance the status and image of that area!

Curriculum

Whatever the nature of your subject, you will be expected to work to a certain pattern; you will need to be aware of the requirements, the levels of progress required and the means of assessing that progress. All these factors will impose a structure on your work and consequently upon the relationships you build with your pupils. The knowledge that a particular individual is failing to achieve a set target, combined with the information you possess regarding the personality and ability of that person, will enable you to formulate strategies for success. The selection of material from that which is available to you and the preparation of schemes of work suitable for your pupils will be a direct result of that knowledge.

In conclusion: it will be seen that a large number of influences exist within (and outside) a school, some physical, others psychological, but all with physical effects on the way you organise your classes. The key factor is observation, followed by early action to make use of the information you have received on this 'hidden agenda' within a school. The behaviours and attitudes of your pupils are all influenced by these factors, and it is only by being aware of them that you will be able to be effective in your teaching.

CHAPTER 2

Creating an Effective Working Atmosphere

Let us assume that you have been appointed to an average sized Comprehensive school with, say, 900 pupils. As a probationary teacher you will be allocated a timetable slightly less than you expect to teach in your later career; expect to teach around 70% of the timetable your main professional grade colleagues will be following.

It is likely that you will be asked to teach some periods of a subject which is not your own specialism. It may be more than that in some smaller secondary schools where the curriculum is more restricted due to staff size. Therefore, as well as struggling with the application of your subject area to practical purpose, you will also be asked to teach a subject which may not even be your subsidiary subject and your knowledge may not be greater than that of your own experiences following an exam course at school yourself. In addition to this, it is quite possible that you will be asked to carry out the duties of a form tutor. Some schools call this a group tutor or, in a vertical system such as a house type organisation, a house tutor. This would involve the administrative tasks associated with keeping your register accurately maintained plus, in many schools, the teaching of a pastoral programme of lessons during tutor time. We will return to this later in Chapter Five.

Many schools now appoint new staff as a subject specialist and form tutor, giving the pastoral role an equal status to that of subject teacher. In the authors' view this is an excellent concept as the school thereby commits itself to treating the pastoral and academic curricula as closely related areas, which indeed they are. As a result you are quite likely to find that you have much to think about. During the first few weeks of your career, at least, you will feel under very great pressure and any concern about this must not be regarded as any sign of weakness or failure since all teachers experience this at the beginning. Suffice it to say that the key to overcoming this is the organisation of your classroom in such a way that your teaching can be economical in time and effort, be effective and enjoyable simultaneously. By taking into account practical factors such as the way you lay out your teaching area, the way you seat your pupils and the manner in which you make use of existing fixed equipment and resources, you will find that the feeling of being overwhelmed by the situation will be diminished. All experienced teachers either achieve this state over a period of months or years or, in extreme cases, adopt an attitude which allows them to ignore pressure. These latter colleagues will be easy to recognise in the staffroom: many will be towards the end of their careers, but beware of categorising your colleagues. It is often part of staffroom banter for teachers to adopt a cynical or 'world weary' pose when relaxing at break or lunchtime. Those same teachers before a class of children may be completely different. It always pays to maintain an open mind.

You will be able to 'gear' certain factors about your situation to your way of working, others will be out of your control. Firstly, the physical environment, the classroon to which you are allocated, will have features difficult to change, others will be totally immovable. Positions of doors and windows, chalkboards, power sockets and cupboards will dictate how you organise your room. However, unless you are teaching as a member of a team, experiencing the assistance of a support teacher in your classroom (to work with less able children) you are in a position of great personal freedom as a classroom teacher.

Constraints

It would be helpful at this stage to consider some of the external factors which will dictate your teaching style to a certain degree. Since your classes will be allocated to you by your Head of Department or Faculty, you will have little choice in respect of the pupils you will be required to teach. A good departmental head will attempt to spread classes regarded as difficult, often allocating such groups to him/herself; however, it is not unknown for a probationary teacher to be allocated such a group. In these circumstances it ought to be possible to resolve the situation by negotiation, but in more extreme cases, it is not. Then there is little option but to accept the situation and treat it positively. Although there is no guarantee of this such classes can often turn out to be the most rewarding in the long run, providing you remain positive and persevere.

The school to which you have been appointed will organise the teaching in one of the following three systems:

(1) Setting

This is where pupils are allocated to groups according to their ability with a 'top' group consisting of the pupils regarded as being the most academically able and motivated, followed by several others in a descending order of ability to a sump group. This last one can fairly be assumed to consist of those pupils who are less able, poorly motivated and may include examples of behaviourally disturbed pupils. This is closest to the once accepted norm of streaming and is common in secondary schools in the fourth year and above, even in those which have adopted an 'all-ability' organisation further down the school.

(2) Banding

It is possible to regard this as a development of setting. In this system pupils are grouped much more loosely in terms of ability and there is scope for pupil movement between bands. It is common for parallel groups to be created to expedite this, but there may still be a hierarchical effect. Consequently a 'sump' group still exists in this system, possibly a pair of banded sump groups. There may well be teachers in your school who are extremely talented with less well motivated pupils and who are able to extract excellent results from them. Equally there may not be any such person and these groups are taught in rotation year by year, so that all the staff within a department are able to gain experience of all abilities of pupil. Obviously, this arrangement would be approached enthusiastically by some staff, less so by others. One effect of the banding system is that pupils will be taught together throughout the school day. The advantages of this might be that pupils know each other better socially and might be less inhibited in involving themselves in some types of classroom experience. On the other hand, such a situation might cause problems for the inexperienced teacher who is unaware of the already established social dynamics of the group, a point explored further in the appendices.

In both setting and banded systems, it is likely that special needs children will be taught in two further ways superimposed over one or both of the above systems. Either they will be withdrawn into special needs classes, where they will be taught by staff with specialist training who will follow a 'watered down' version of the school curriculum (particularly in the post-14 years), or pupils will experience an alternative curriculum geared to their individual needs. This, of course, presupposes small groups. Alternatively, special needs pupils may well remain within mainstream groups, receiving help from support teachers who will be present in your classroom to assist them. These staff may be specialist teachers, but it is quite common for all staff in some schools to support other colleagues for the occasional lesson in a week, often to fill out their teaching timetable. This is more likely if that person is a specialist in a minority subject area. It is therefore possible that you might act as support to another colleague for one or two lessons per week, or receive support help yourself, particularly if your group contains 'statemented' pupils. These pupils have been assessed under the 1981 Education Act as requiring special help and a 'statement' of their needs is prepared by the L.E.A. – hence their designation.

Both setting and banding create fewer organisational challenges than all-ability since the pupils are of approximately the same ability and the pitch of your approach will be more consistently delivered to all.

(3) All-Ability

This is a development of mixed-ability teaching which has existed in some authorities for many years. In the past, special needs pupils have been extracted leaving groups of all abilities mixed together, except those of low ability. More recently the trend, as outlined above, has been to incorporate special needs pupils into mainstream teaching and therefore groups became truly all-ability. This system creates many inherent difficulties in teaching organisation, but may be regarded as a logical extension of the Comprehensive ideal. Indeed, it has to be stated that our primary school colleagues have operated this system for many years with great success. The pressures of exam teaching have tended to create philosophical disagreement over the efficacy of the approach in the secondary sector but many schools operate the system successfully. All-ability teaching is the most challenging of all forms of classroom organisation, and therefore it requires individual approaches, a structure plan well in advance and the use of material pitched at widely differing levels. The greatest danger of this system lies in the fact that there is a tendency to direct the material to the average student allowing the less able to flounder and the academically able to underachieve. Support teaching, discussed in a further chapter, is essential to the well-being of an all-ability class.

In practice, secondary schools often use a combination of all three types of teaching rather than exclusively one of them. It is common for the first year in a Comprehensive school to be organised on all-ability lines, indeed this is becoming the norm. Many schools extend this to cover the years 7–9 but maintain setting in years 10 and 11. In 11–18 schools with small sixth forms, the teaching often returns to all ability with self selection by subject choice and success or otherwise at G.C.S.E. level. Therefore you are likely to encounter a mixture of the above systems. Let us now look at the way these methods of organisation and the subject taught may affect your classroom organisation.

Classroom organisation

The G.C.S.E. exam has introduced pupil-centred activities to all subject areas. The effect of this has been to diminish the use of didactic class teaching, although it must not be imagined that there is now no place for it. In fact you are likely to be using a variety of methods. However, your subject specialism will dictate the manner in which you will work in your classroom: a Science practical lesson must be organised in a manner different to that of an English or Modern Languages oral lesson. How are the pupils to be seated? Where will you stand? Will the pupils work in groups? Some of these considerations can be explored by considering the examples in Practical Task One at the end of this chapter. You might find it useful to match some of these with differing seating arrangements.

There is, of course, no right answer, but certain arrangements are clearly more appropriate to particular lessons. Obviously group work will dictate pupils sitting in groups, the size of which will vary according to class size. For example, a Technology lesson requires the use of fixed equipment, e.g. computer, benches, machines, causing the seating layout in a class to have a completely different character to, say, that of a year ten G.C.S.E. English group where pupils might be seated in groups of four or five around large tables.

An oral lesson in any subject could be delivered in a variety of modes depending upon the subject material. A discussion with the teacher leading might be organised around a semi-circle, whilst a group discussion would involve pupils being split into groups.

The success, or otherwise, of a particular lesson depends as much upon the way in which you deliver it as the manner in which you prepare your materials. It must be said, however, that there is no correct or all embracing methodology. It is up to you to select the appropriate method for you and the way you wish to deliver a subject. There has been a movement in recent years to more pupil-centred approaches with an 'active learning' content. This implies that the pupils are required to work in groups on planned tasks with the teacher playing the role of adviser rather than didactic leader. In the right situation this is a most effective method of learning, but there has been a tendency recently to assume that this is the only 'correct' method of creating a learning atmosphere. Education is as subject to fashion as are other areas of human activity, but the important fact to bear in mind is that you should have a whole range of teaching and learning strategies at your disposal. In this context, didactic teaching, 'led' lessons and so on all have their place.

The knowledge that you have of your pupils' background will affect the way in which you see them. In some cases this information will be highly relevant, in others, not. Other staff will comment on a particular child either positively or adversely when they become aware that you teach him/her. By all means take this into account but use your own judgement too and give every pupil a chance until they have regularly behaved in a particular way with you. It is worth pointing out at this stage that all behaviours have a reason and if a pupil behaves in an undesirable manner and you have no pre-knowledge of his/her background, always try to find out as much as you can from the form tutor or, with permission, go to the pupils' record cards.

Building up information about pupils is an important part of a teacher's role. Let us assume now that you have quite a complete picture of your class. The process of building up this information is the subject of Practical Task Two (see page 26) which will enable you to construct a typical group of children matching names with known behavioural traits, information relating to home situations and academic backgrounds. Furthermore, the group is all-ability and year ten following a G.C.S.E. course in your subject. The group is mixed race and representative of all social backgrounds. This is the type of combination found in many Comprehensive schools.

By this stage you should be thinking of your pupils as individuals. It is pointless preparing a lesson without knowing your pupils if you aim to maximise individual potential. Teaching a lesson to a class you do not know is common, however, as in covering for absent colleagues, or undertaking the role of supply teacher. In these conditions the aim is different in that you are occupying the class gainfully and with the minimum of disruption for pupil or teacher. With your class you can afford to be more exacting. Plan your lessons with sufficient material to occupy both the pupil who progresses slowly and the academic child who finishes set tasks early. Knowing the standard each child is capable of gaining enables you to engineer your strategies effectively. Additionally, treating each child as an individual rather than just a member of a class will enhance your relationship with them.

When pupils work in groups you are more likely to gain more knowledge of them as individuals because the teacher moves around them and talks in turn with each child. This is more difficult when a class is being taught in a traditional, formal manner. It is necessary to be aware that adolescent pupils particularly are sometimes reluctant to involve themselves in discussion on a more than one-to-one basis, for fear of embarrassment in front of their peers.

Behavioural management

Although the aim is to create an atmosphere of calm in your classroom in which all your pupils will flourish and develop, it is helpful to be able to deal with challenges to your authority as soon as they arise and before they develop to a dangerous level. One of the commonest difficulties faced by all teachers is the problem of the very talkative pupil. Strategies in dealing with this might include (a) separation, (b) directing their energies, (c) using the talkativeness by harnessing it to an oral lesson. Two minutes' light hearted banter with you at the beginning of the lesson is preferable to a whole lesson spent talking to friends and consequently causing you stress. Listed below are a selection of possible situations with which you might have to deal:

- a pupil who regularly fails to hand in homework
- a pupil who is shy but needs an oral grade to gain the G.C.S.E. which she/he deserves
- the pupil with a low boredom threshold
- the ingratiating pupil who curries favour with you
- the pupil who writes on desks
- theft of an item or money from the classroom
- the pupil who mimics you
- the pupil who interferes with other pupils' work

There is, of course, no one correct answer to these problems but you may find it interesting to relate them to the pupils you know. What would be your strategy if one of your pupils began to write on the desk regularly? Naturally your plan of action will be influenced by individual traits, academic potential, nuisance value to the rest of the class, frequency of behaviour, etc. However, the most important question to ask yourself is: what is causing the behaviour? An understanding of this will help you form your strategy.

Crisis Management

The above situations are likely to occur from time to time in the most regulated of classrooms and can be approached calmly and thoughtfully. Unfortunately the often volatile nature of teenage behaviour can lead to outbursts of unacceptable behaviour with any teacher; therefore it is quite possible that you will have to deal with such an outburst, maintaining your calm and preventing it from overwhelming the lesson, the class and, ultimately, yourself.

In your first week of teaching it is quite likely that situations will arise which you will need to handle without losing self control. In fact the importance of staying calm cannot be overstated! It is most unlikely that the following situations could happen simultaneously, but they are worth considering as typical examples of things which might occur during your average working day.

Consider briefly the amount of time you would have to resolve these problems while maintaining a calm, organised atmosphere. You are likely to be constrained by time in making these decisions and therefore you may find it helpful to try the timed crisis exercises given below:

Give yourself precisely thirty seconds to deal with each of these, asking a friend to time you. This is to simulate the time pressure you may be under when dealing with such situations.

	Incident	*Your Response*
(1)	Not enough chairs in the room	
(2)	You have brought the wrong set of exercise books	
(3)	Pupil is violently sick	
(4)	Class refuse to do the work you had planned to do	

Analyse your response; what are you thinking and what potential consequences were you expecting?

These are typical of the sorts of incidents or problems which require a speedy decision; of course it is unlikely that they will all occur in any one lesson, although a combination of several of them might. The most important point to bear in mind is to remain as calm as possible under pressure, to have alternative activities or work in mind in case anything goes wrong, and to remember above all else that these things happen to all of us; all your colleagues will have learned to cope with such incidents, often making mistakes along the way. It is worthwhile stressing that these incidents are an everyday part of school life!

Occasionally, a more serious incident will occur. Usually help is not far away and you should never hesitate to ask for it. However, the following are taken from the experiences of the writers at different stages of their careers:

- stray dogs run into the room, fighting
- angry parent appears at classroom door
- pupil lights a cigarette at the back of class
- exam correspondent made a mistake over exam entries for your group which are due today
- pupil has a fit
- teacher storms in, picks on a pupil who is totally surprised by the incident and protests his innocence
- experiment in Science blows up and catches fire

Some of these require immediate help, for instance the accident in Science. However, the angry parent clearly requires a different strategy. In this case your aim is first to get the parent away from your room and then to get the problem sorted out. This might involve escorting the parent to reception and arranging for a senior member of staff to hear their complaint. Clearly some of these can be resolved by an instantaneous decision, others by negotiation or by referring the matter to more senior colleagues.

The guiding principle behind your actions during these incidents should be to remain calm. You cannot possibly hope to deal with some of these incidents yourself and you should seek help quickly from a colleague in an adjacent room. If your room is isolated, send a trusted pupil to either a classroom where you know someone will be or to the school office. In the case of the experiment exploding, the school would have to be evacuated by means of the fire drill. You would break the glass *after* getting your pupils out of the room. Then, and only then, should you make an attempt to fight the fire. The safety of your pupils and yourself must be paramount. With the exam entries mistake, the fault is not yours but you should not be concerned with apportioning blame; instead, supply the necessary information as quickly as possible.

Always be aware of your limitations and do not hesitate to enlist the support of other colleagues; you will be soon find out who you can trust and who to avoid. Remember it is *not a sign of failure to ask for help*, providing that on other occasions you have made every effort yourself to resolve the situation first. No one has failed a probationary period as a result of asking for assistance.

This chapter has dealt with two main areas. The aim has been firstly, to raise your awareness of the dynamics of groups of pupils and to demonstrate that by understanding them and planning your lesson organisation accordingly, you will prevent trouble arising. Secondly, we have suggested that when it is necessary to cope with crisis situations, you should develop the capacity to remain calm, deal with those situations that you can cope with and request assistance for those with which you cannot.

PRACTICAL TASK ONE

Consider the following types of lesson:
(a) An all-ability year nine Science group: practical lesson.
(b) An all-ability year nine P.S.E. (Personal and Social Education) lesson with a video being shown.
(c) A 'mid range' year ten G.C.S.E. English lesson: banded group: oral lesson.
(d) A P.E. lesson you have been asked to cover for an absent colleague. Boys and girls are mixed together and the lesson is held in a classroom owing to inclement weather.
(e) C.D.T. (Craft, Design and Technology) lesson: year nine: all-ability. This is a lesson of theory as your usual room cannot be used since practical G.C.S.E. exam is taking place there.
(f) A settled year eleven lesson: Modern Languages: a listening test: oral work and worksheets.

Now evaluate the following methods of seating and grouping pupils (Fig. 1) and decide which is appropriate to each lesson type (a)–(f).

Figure 1.

(1) Pupils seated in a row:

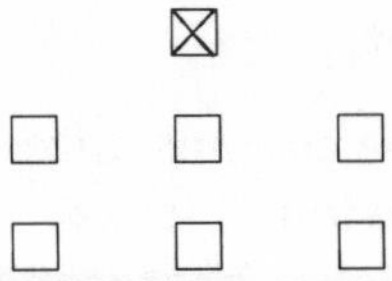

(2) Pupils seated in a semi-circle:

(3) Pupils seated in groups:

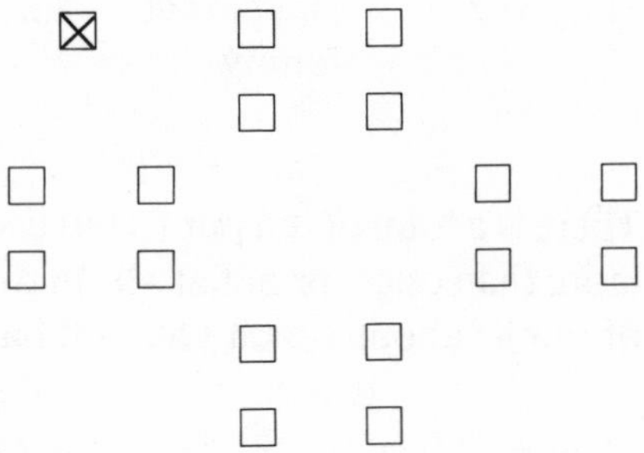

(4) Pupils seated in groups:

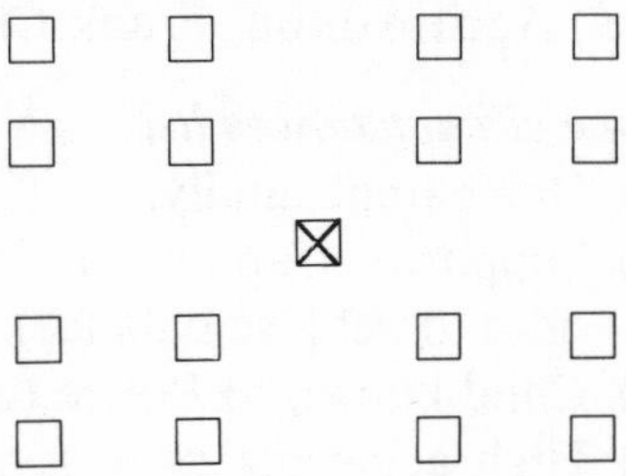

(5) Pupils seated in the 'round':

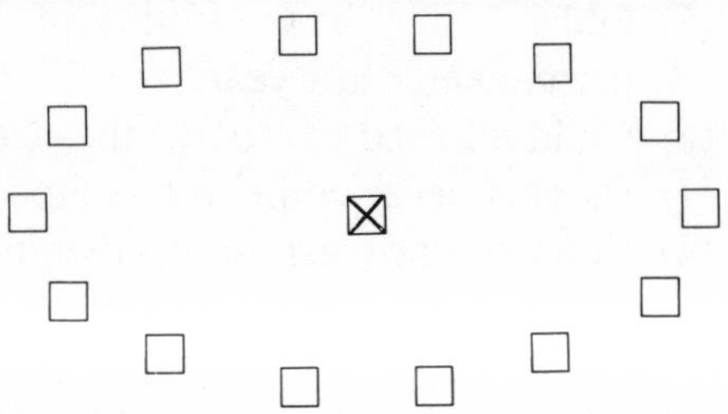

Key: teacher ⊠ ; pupils ☐

PRACTICAL TASK TWO

Arrange the following ten pupils' names with **ONE** statement from each list of:

- Home circumstances
- Behavioural traits
- Academic background

A complete picture is built up on each pupil. You may mix them in any order achieving, for example, the following result:

Name	Home Circumstances	Behavioural Traits	Academic Background
Mary Inge	one parent family	known epileptic	poor writing, weak in basic spelling & maths

There is a total of ten pupils but each piece of information may be used more than once, or not at all. In this way you will have created a group of pupils about which you will have a wide background knowedge.

Names: Mary Inge, Michelle Graham, Orkendi Mazra, Natasha Hussein, John Ashe, Alan Craddock, Marion Komalski, Armand Patel, April Ashton, Frank Clemson.

Home circumstances list
 (1) One parent family.
 (2) Supportive family – no known problems. (Use this more than once to achieve balance).
 (3) Child known to Police for theft and vandalism.
 (4) High achieving professional parents with high expectations of child.
 (5) Older sister had reputation for disruption and suspended permanently last year.
 (6) Child allowed to 'roam' the streets at night.
 (7) Parents never come in to school.
 (8) Child recently arrived to live in this country. Parents and pupil unaware of school's expectations.
 (9) Suspected sexual abuse. No proof.
(10) Impoverished background but very caring and supportive parents.
(11) Parents support school and are members of P.T.A.

(12) Mother known to have deserted family and father is unlikely to cope.
(13) Parent supportive and always willing to come into school and discuss problems.
(14) Child adopted and difficult to handle. Parents struggle but want to help.
(15) Child lives with mother and stepfather, who has brought two children from a previous marriage. This pupil fights them regularly.
(16) Family has huge debts and electricity switched off yesterday.
(17) Regularly in trouble with Police. Court appearance for assault.
(18) Parents supportive in theory but always side with child in any school problem.
(19) Has been seen by Educational Psychologist at mother's request as she is worried that child is incapable of forming adequate social relationships.
(20) Parents hate and despise teachers and make this known to their children.

Behavioural traits (use singly, or as appropriate, in multiples)

(1) No discernible traits.
(2) Damages others' property.
(3) Pleasant, open pupil.
(4) Would work well whatever the environment.
(5) Bursts into tears, timid.
(6) Truants.
(7) Easily led.
(8) Fails to follow instructions, gossips.
(9) Packs away early.
(10) Never has a pen.
(11) Pleasant but 'dreamy'.
(12) Lethargic, works very slowly.
(13) Works well in one-to-one situations.
(14) Statemented.
(15) Fails to do detentions.
(16) Always finishes first.
(17) Well motivated and keen.
(18) Physically threatening.
(19) Deaf but will not admit it.
(20) Orally confident but written work is weak.

Academic background

(1) Very bright and astute. Quickly finds and exploits teacher weaknesses.
(2) Exceptionally able and will achieve excellent G.C.S.E. results in most subjects.
(3) Poor handwriting and weak in basic spelling and arithmetic.
(4) Works hard and achieves an average standard.
(5) Dyslexic, teachers asked to make allowances. Is receiving help.
(6) Slow worker, below average ability.
(7) Works satisfactorily.
(8) Often requires and receives help from a support teacher. Struggles with reading which impairs progress in all areas.
(9) Has developed a lazy streak. Able but not reaching potential.
(10) Low boredom threshold, low attainment, poor progress.
(11) Has difficulty in organising him/herself.
(12) Excellent in practical subjects, does not enjoy written work.
(13) Academically poor, hates work, refuses to cooperate, progress slow.
(14) Average but could achieve much better results with pressure.
(15) Performs well in exams and tests. G.C.S.E. assessments poor due to lack of motivation and poor attendance.
(16) Difficulty with basic reading, comprehension and punctuation.
(17) Quick thinking.
(18) Underachieving.
(19) Poor homework record.
(20) Bright but missed two terms owing to glandular fever last year.

You should now have ten pupils with a summary of all known information. In fact you will be better informed than you are likely to be in reality, at least initially. You may well find that your class does not reflect the average group owing to a high incidence of behavioural disorders or deprivation, but this may provoke questions of stereotyping or the inadvisability of relying too much upon information received indirectly. It may be of interest also to analyse why you allocated a particular behavioural trait to a given pupil; did you show a sexist approach by 'creating' a female pupil with stereotyped attributes? Were your representatives from any ethnic minority displaying expected behaviours, or academically underachieving? It is important that, as teachers, we are honest with ourselves and come to terms with any prejudice about any pupil which we might hold. An open mind is a pre-requisite of the successful teacher.

PRACTICAL TASK THREE

(1) Take a sheet of paper and draw a BOX SHAPE. This represents a classroom. Draw a door and indicate window areas. We suggest using a piece of A4 sized paper, the dimensions of the room being 25cm × 10cm. (Fig. 2).

(2) Cut out 10 squares and write the name of each pupil on them. You now have a collection of pupils (the background information upon which you have already noted).

(3) Seat these pupils in your classroom, taking care to avoid undesirable mixes.

(4) Look at the selection of lesson types (a)–(f) discussed in Task One.

(5) Take each one in turn:

   1 Does your seating plan alter significantly with each lesson?

   2 Which of your pupils is paramount in your mind when thinking about each lesson type?

   3 Which pupils require obvious encouragement in a particular lesson?

Figure 2. This is your allocated classroom.

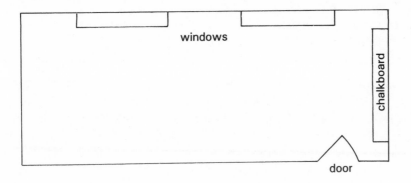

CHAPTER 3

Preparation of Work

Imagine your first 'proper' lesson in front of a class of lively, though not necessarily enthusiastic, mixed-ability eleven year olds. You have prepared your fifty minute lesson as thoroughly as you think is necessary, and are fully aware that a member of H.M.I. is wandering the school on this particular morning.

It is Mathematics and the lesson, graph work, entails a brief introductory demonstration to the whole class followed by the distribution of work sheets, gummed coloured papers, scissors, rulers and pens.

The work sheet begins with relatively simple examples of the work which you have introduced while, as pupils progress through their work, the examples demand more deliberation and the application of ideas covered previously.

After twenty minutes the room is buzzing with activity; the introduction and distribution of equipment have gone extremely well.

Within minutes of pupils working alone, however, there are problems. Some claim to have done the work at primary school; several have found the whole concept too daunting but did not make this clear during your introductory remarks, and a final few, with apparent glee, have only completed the last three examples, perfectly, because their grasp of the work was so clear that they saw little point in plodding through the simpler questions. At that point you espy, walking purposefully down the corridor, the H.M.I. . . .

The example is not totally apocryphal: one of the authors suffered a similar fate on his first teaching practice with a class of primary pupils. Fortunately, the classroom teacher was present and, with her experience, was able to present work to the pupils which productively occupied those who appeared not to need any further work on the topic, while providing a breathing space to help those who were in desperate need of further guidance. Fortunately, the H.M.I. did not enter the room.

With experience of classroom management the situation described above would not be too daunting but it presents, in a nutshell, many of the difficulties and worries which confront the inexperienced teacher. Put simply these might be considered as follows:

Is the prepared work:

● relevant to all pupils' needs?
● presented in a way which will interest all, providing basic understanding for the weak but a stimulus to stretch the most able?
● sufficient to fill the allocated time?

On a day-to-day basis such considerations are possibly the chief concerns of the student, probationer or inexperienced teacher but such an approach is to put the cart a considerable way in front of the horse.

Other factors are of greater importance when beginning to plan the delivery of a course. Such factors as the overall curriculum planning of the school, the faculty or department; the amount of time allocated to the subject in a particular school year; the availability of resources; the setting or grouping structure of classes and so on will have a strong influence on the teacher's planning strategy in both the long and short term. Obviously, the arrival of the National Curriculum with its clearly laid out attainment targets at each of the key stages will have a major bearing on what you will teach. It may not influence the delivery of the work in the lesson but it is inevitable that it will influence, to some extent, what is taught at what stage.

Long term aims

Let us begin, however, with consideration of a very simple but most significant factor which should be our major priority before undertaking the planning of a syllabus or course. This is quite simply: 'What are we hoping that our pupils will be gaining from our teacher?' Depending upon the subject taught, the following might be the major long term aims:

(1) The obtaining and retention of knowledge.
(2) The acquisition of skills which are pertinent to the subject.
(3) The ability to apply both this knowledge and these skills in given situations.

(4)   The development of pupils' awareness of the relevance of learning to their lives.
(5)   To provide opportunities for pupils to acquire values, social skills and an awareness of cultural issues.
(6)   The preparation, particularly as pupils mature and reach the final years of schooling, for their role in the adult world which they are soon to enter.

Such a list of aims is not exhaustive but, in the authors' view, they provide a basic framework in which, if any element is ignored, we might be considered to be failing the youngsters in our charge. Indeed, the Education Reform Act 1988 (E.R.A.) provides two principles which subsume the above aims. It states that the curriculum of a school should:

● promote the spiritual, moral, cultural, mental and physical development of pupils at the school and of society.
● prepare such pupils for the opportunities, responsibilities and experiences of adult life.

The importance of these aims will receive different weighting in different subject areas. It is quite realistic to anticipate that a similar aim might be covered by two subject areas in completely different ways.
    For instance, let us take a nebulous theme such as 'Justice' and consider both how different departments might treat it and how it satisfies the above aims. Working on the assumption that we are dealing with a fairly bright class of year ten pupils, the theme might be treated as follows by Geography, History and English:

Geography

As part of Economic Geography pupils might consider the distribution of wealth throughout the world, the relative poverty of the Third World and the affluence of the Western World. Such work might involve reasoning exercises on causes of such distribution and how the imbalances might be corrected.

History

Pupils might be working on 'The Wild West'. Such work would include a consideration of the causes of disputes between the

American Indian and settlers over land. Once more, such work might involve pupils in looking at the justice of each case.

English

To Kill a Mockingbird, a novel by Harper Lee in which a negro is wrongly accused of the rape of a white girl and, while being proved innocent is still found guilty, might be read. Such reading might lead to a consideration of justice in society. Debates, discursive essays, creative writing and so on, might well result from this.

Thus, when we analyse the work being done by three different departments, we see both the satisfaction of short term objectives and the relevance to long term aims as listed above, and particularly the consideration of moral and cultural values in preparation for adult life.

With increasing frequency, cross-curricular threads are being developed as T.V.E.I., Expressive Arts, Balanced Science and Humanities become the vehicles for teaching many of the subjects which previously held an individual status in the curriculum. It might be that, in your school, such developments will necessitate your considering the wider relevance of your specialised subject to a framework based on the long term objectives of several departments working together. Such an exercise is of value as it provides an opportunity to see what you do in the classroom in a wider context.

Short term objectives

Each year, however, and in many subjects and schools, each term will demand a less far-sighted view. Pupils at different stages of development will require work which not only fulfils long term aims but which satisfies short term objectives dictated by different syllabus requirements, skills to be acquired and knowledge to be learned. The National Curriculum, for instance, will make great demands of this nature with attainment targets set and assessments by various methods at key stages three (11–14) and four (14–16).

Thus, on arriving in a new school, the inexperienced teacher might expect to find, in a well organised department, a syllabus which offers a guide to the type of work which each year group should be completing and a summary of the main objectives, in terms of learned skills or knowledge, which pupils will be expected to acquire.

On the other hand, it must be acknowledged that some departments simply indicate what is done in each year or term. Hence, the probationary Biology teacher who arrives in school to be told, 'In the second year, we do the digestive system', will need to probe much more deeply, not only to glean more information about the actual content of this part of the course but also to discover what the objectives are behind teaching it. With the knowledge of these short term objectives it is possible for the teacher, particularly as experience grows, to decide the best order in which to approach aspects of the topic and the most effective means of presentation for the benefit of his/her pupils.

One of the most common cries from disaffected or challenging youngsters is 'Why are we doing this?' A swift, confident response, made in a straightforward jargon-free manner indicating the purpose behind the work, will immediately enhance your standing in the classroom. Requests for such information should not always be seen, however, as attempts to undermine your authority; pupils are becoming increasingly critical 'consumers' of what they are offered. It is in neither their, nor our, interests for them to be told to do it because it is there. A clear indication of our objectives and, if necessary, an account of how these objectives satisfy part of the school's or society's long term aims, helps pupils to understand the relevance of their education.

Now you are confident about your six week course of two fifty minute sessions each week and clear in your mind about the presentation of the work you intend to cover, and the class awaits your opening gambits. It is often within the following fifteen minutes or so that the management of the classroom is most severely challenged. While you may have prepared the lesson down to the last detail with a variety of activities, clear steps for pupils to follow and carefully considered questions and follow-up work, the unknown quantity is the reaction of the class. The ability to handle a class who draw you away from the immediate point, either deliberately or through innocent interest is of paramount importance. Again, confident and careful thought should ensure that such a situation is not detrimental to the lesson and, indeed, might well enhance it. The two most necessary factors to bear in mind are:

(1) Ensure that you remain firmly in control of any unexpected developments. Should the lesson be moving in the wrong direction and you feel uncomfortable, draw the pupils' attentions back to the main issue in a calm way.

(2)   Accept that there is nothing amiss in 'drifting' from the point but as far as possible attempt to relate the unexpected discussion to the key objective of the lesson.

The ability to handle these situations often comes easily to more experienced teachers. As in all areas of classroom management, to ask for and accept advice from senior colleagues in the preparation of your objectives and the work necessary to meet these is not a sign of inadequacy. Many of your ideas will have been tried before by long standing teachers and their advice might well help you to gain confidence in your ability to plan effective schemes of work.

Now, in order to examine the relevance of aims and objectives to your classroom management procedures, see Practical Task Four, (page 47).

Pupils' needs

So far in this chapter, we have only considered what the teacher intends to cover in helping to provide a broadly balanced education. It is, however, of obvious but paramount importance to consider the academic needs and development of the pupils both as a class and, as far as possible, as individuals. The teacher armed to the teeth with academic qualifications is of little help to pupils if he/she is not able to present the subject in such a way that their understanding of it is enhanced.

The organisation of teaching groups has been considered earlier but a prior knowledge of the type of group which you are to teach will aid you in organising appropriate work. While it is wrong to approach groups with preconceived ideas and prejudices about their academic ability, it must be acknowledged that setting or banded classes will help the teacher to understand what types of academic need he/she is likely to encounter. Thus, for example, teaching class one of six setted classes will, from the outset, entail a different approach to teaching your subject matter from the approach you might make to class six. Of greatest difficulty when considering pupils' academic needs is the all-ability class in that it is impossible to make any pre-judgements about the suitability of your teaching to the whole group. Thorough knowledge of any group's academic need comes only with time spent in the company of that group, but to account for the differences in an all-ability group requires careful monitoring of the individual pupil. It might well be necessary to set work at different levels but this is a difficult task until pupils' needs are known.

It will be necessary to discover, as a first principle, what the pupils already know. This information might well be available to you if the group is one which has been taught together previously in the school. Assuming that the department has a syllabus for the previous year's work and that pupils have a report, Record of Achievement, or test results, you are already on the way to knowing what pupils should already know and a brief resumé, in an appropriate way at the outset of the proposed topic, will provide an indication of whether further revision might be needed before the new work can be begun. First year pupils in the secondary school, however, pose a slightly different problem. Unless the school in which you find yourself is exceptionally small, it is likely that pupils will arrive from a variety of feeder schools; probably each of these will have offered different knowledge, expectations and methods of working. In such cases it is best to begin from a basic starting point which leaves no child at a disadvantage but from which you should try to move on as quickly as possible in order to avoid disaffection and boredom at such an early and crucial stage.

The social dynamics of the group might also influence the apparent, if not real, academic needs of the pupils. Consider, for instance, in an all-ability class whether the more intelligent pupils willingly help those who struggle to achieve. It is accepted that the key to the understanding of work is often revealed in one's ability to impart that knowledge to a third party (examinations are, after all, only a formalised method of doing this) and if it is possible to harness a group's social cohesion to the benefit of all at times, this is a ploy worth using. It should, however, be used sparingly as pupils can become convinced that the teacher is avoiding his/her responsibilities to individuals in the groups even if this is not actually true. Consider, too, the child who intimidates others and makes the less able feel threatened if they ask for help or insidiously causes the more able to work at a slower rate than they wish. This latter character might be difficult to detect but he or she is capable of dictating pupils' needs subtly and such situations should be watched for. Perhaps the most apparent indicators are when the written work which pupils produce reflects achievement which is not commensurate with their apparent ability in other aspects of work or where they finish early but fail to make it apparent to the teacher.

The speed at which pupils work when completing tasks is another indicator of whether you are satisfying a pupil's academic needs. If the work is completed with haste but quite satisfactorily in a short time and with no difficulty, it might be that pupils have been occupied but not stretched towards achieving their potential. Undoubtedly some would enjoy simply filling time but this fails to fulfil their true needs. On the other hand, the pupil who does not concentrate and constantly needs attention to help him to complete work might be having extreme difficulty – the work is more than stretching him, it is destroying his interest and confidence.

Other factors which need to be considered at various times are whether pupils are following the course in order to take a public examination at the end; or where the course fits into an overall scheme of study. A pupil who has decided not to take Drama as an examination option subject in year ten might show little motivation for the work towards the end of year nine. Pupils might reveal a great deal of stereotyping in the behaviour they have learned at home, for instance, some boys see no relevance in studying Textiles. Such attitudes obviously need to be challenged, forthrightly, calmly and with reason but the example reveals one of the problems when considering pupils' academic needs; they are not always aware of their needs nor can they take the long term view of a broad education which we as teachers need to consider as our starting point.

It is, therefore, necessary for the classroom teacher to balance very many factors if he/she is to do full justice to all the demands which are made on him/her. The syllabus provides the stimulus and objectives while the needs of pupils and their social grouping influence the method of presentation. How is it possible to square the circle?

As has already been made clear, your objectives and work schemes will have been developed before you are able to present them to the pupils. Once the scheme of work has been started it is necessary to be open-minded about varying your approach or materials as you respond to the ways in which pupils react to the topic which you present. It may be necessary to compromise in various ways, for instance:

- If the pupils' powers of concentration will not allow sustained work in one direction for more than thirty minutes, while the topic you are dealing with is certain to take a one hour lesson, it might well be necessary to think out an approach which will allow you to deal with it in two stages or two different ways.
- If your topic requires research by the pupils but past experience shows that they do not use the school or public library, it might be

necessary to engineer a situation where your lesson takes place in the school library or where resources are brought from the school library to the classroom.

- Your scheme of work might require group work but after ten minutes it is clear that pupils, for whatever reason, are not satisfying your objectives for the lesson. In such circumstances, resorting to pair-work or individual work followed by group discussion might be the solution.
- Where pupils are simply not able to cope with the demands of the work in one of your lessons. You may have to simplify the work immediately, which entails swift action in organisation, stimulus materials and teaching method.

The list of possible compromises is endless but it is better to modify your approach in the interests of both pupils and the lesson content rather than rigidly adhere to your first idea regardless of the problems you encounter. At the same time, the objectives of the lesson and syllabus demands should not, of course, be altered. Once again, enlist the experience of others as an aid in this. Many seasoned teachers feel the atmosphere of the classroom, can sense where difficulties lie and, through their experience, immediately change approach to help their children. A form tutor or Head of House or Year, knowing the pupils, might well be able to advise on abilities, concentration levels, social groupings and so on which are bound to affect your classroom practice, no matter how well prepared you are.

To consider some of the above principles in practice when faced with a course to organise and pupils' needs to accommodate, look at Practical Task Five at the end of the chapter.

Teaching methods

In the previous chapter we considered the physical and organisational constraints which might influence the physical setting of your class group. The teaching method which you adopt will need to take account of these too, along with your objectives, pupils' academic needs and your own comfort in approaching your class. At some point in the staffroom you might hear a comment not dissimilar to this:

'Kids today, don't want to learn. You can talk until you're blue in the face and at the end of it all they still don't understand. Or, they sit and doodle when I say take notes. A clip round the ear would do them good, or the cane. They'd sit and listen then.'

The question is, of course, would they 'listen then'? The comment reflects an extremely outmoded view which equates silence, stillness and looking at the teacher with understanding, learning and pupil progress. Perhaps the teacher making such a comment might fit the stereotype of a previous era when teaching method figured less significantly in a teacher's weaponry. Standing in front of a class, made silent by your ability to quieten them and then saying what you wanted to say was often considered enough.

Teaching strategies in the classroom have, however, now grown in importance, as a result of curricular developments such as T.V.E.I., C.P.V.E. the G.C.S.E. examinations and so on. Two examples of the way in which teaching method has changed owing to the latter examination are in the areas of English and Science. In English, the requirement for pupils to complete several oral assessments in a variety of situations which might involve the class, group work, pair work or direct discussion with the teacher has ensured that all English teachers need to formalise methods which facilitate varied oral activities. That is not to say that such activities were not already taking place in classrooms before the advent of G.C.S.E. but that the new examination requirements have made teachers assess what sorts of opportunities for oral work they have presented to pupils. In Science, too, the emphasis on practical activities and practical assessments has influenced the methods of the teacher in the classroom. Once more, Science has always involved practical activities but the assessment procedures of G.C.S.E. have ensured that teachers must consider the ways in which pupils have been involved in such work.

Thus, while didactic teaching methods, active or experiential learning, pupil-centred learning, group work, field work and individual learning programmes have always been teaching methods available to all, it is only relatively recently that we have been encouraged to consider them among the variety of strategies available to us. In fact, the different terms might be considered in two main groups, didactic methods and individualised methods.

Didactic teaching

This method of teaching might be termed 'teacher led'. The teacher has a body of knowledge to impart and sets about explaining, giving notes and summary sheets or reads from textbooks with pupils. He may demonstrate an activity and then allow pupils to repeat it to obtain the same results. At all stages the teacher ostensibly controls what is learned by placing himself at the centre of pupils' learning as a provider of information to be learned in a clearly, closely structured way. Lesson preparation is relatively easy when all follow the same work.

The advantages of this method are that the teacher is fully aware of everything which all pupils are doing. He has clear control of each step in the child's development in his subject and is able to monitor success and failure in a simple but well-defined way. This is probably the method which older teachers identify with as it is a strategy which worked successfully in the era of the tripartite system with streaming and setting for classroom organisation. The reason why is obvious; pupils tended to be in groups of similar ability and, therefore, the teacher had a reasonable idea of what knowledge and skills pupils could handle and at what pace.

The disadvantage of this method is that pupils are treated as clones with little opportunity for individual development or individual enquiry except as an extra for those pupils motivated to show interest outside the formal, classroom atmosphere.

Individual teaching methods

This method actually appears under many guises. Essential to the philosophy behind it, however, is that all pupils are individual, with individual needs and different levels of interest and ability in the subject. Hence, the development of each pupil needs to be monitored individually and the classroom organisation should be structured in such a way that this individuality is allowed for in the learning process. While the teacher introduces the topic, has an aim for the lesson and needs to monitor the progress of pupils, he allows pupils to work from the stimulus material at their own pace to achieve the goal. In such a situation, the teacher is also a provider of information but he will provide it for individuals as and when they need it, acting as a guide and helper as pupils find their own structure for the learning process. A great onus is placed upon the teacher to trust pupils, to be able to assess a pupils' needs and advise quickly so that he may help all pupils during the lesson, and to be able to monitor progress in a situation where all pupils are at different stages. A great awareness of all that is going on in the classroom is vital.

The advantages of such a method are that pupils are treated as individuals, their individual needs are central to the classroom learning experience and that, done properly, the relationship between pupils and teacher is considerably enhanced as a partnership tends to develop. In all-ability situations this method is generally likely to be more successful than the didactic method. To teach all lessons to a class using the same material in the same way for pupils of widely varying abilities and to expect them to achieve similar goals at the same pace is impossible. This method allows for the problem.

The disadvantage is that it may be difficult to find the time to help all pupils as much as they need (a fifty minute lesson for a class of twenty five only allows an average of two minutes per pupil). Consequently, every pupil may not reach the stage that the teacher envisaged.

So, which method is best? The material, the needs of pupils and the experience of the teacher with the class all play a part in influencing your decision. In many respects, it is best to keep an open mind as some situations will demand didactic methods and others will demand individual methods. Let us consider some of these situations.

A second year, all-ability class of 18 pupils is completing a six week course in Creative Textiles as part of an Expressive Arts course within the curriculum. Some basic work has been completed in year one on the various techniques which are relevant to producing a project in the subject. The overall aim of this six week course is the design of an item and its realisation using at least four of the techniques learned in year one. Objectives such as:

- revision of the previous year's work,
- the relevance and suitability of the design work to the overall brief,
- the consideration of the suitability of the textile techniques to the final item,
- the skill of the pupil in using the techniques,
- the sensitive creativity of the individual

are built into this overall aim.

The design brief given to the pupils is to produce an item to wear or hang on the wall based on the theme of 'The Sea'.

As placing oneself at the centre of the learning process and 'controlling' the learning process closely is at the heart of the 'didactic' approach, the teacher might decide to pursue this topic on the following lines:

Lesson one

Revise first year techniques with pupils offering examples to the teacher to write on the board. Following this, pupils and teacher discuss and write down the processes involved in the techniques.

Lesson two

The theme of 'The Sea' is presented to pupils. An outline of the aim is given. Pupils will be expected to design a tropical fish or an aquatic plant from the books the teacher has brought from the library. Pupils complete their basic design, as the teacher monitors their efforts. As all pupils reach a stage where they have almost finished, the teacher states that they are now to produce a picture, to hang on the wall, using their design and four suitable techniques.

Lesson three

A brief reminder of the previous two weeks' work. Pupils are invited to suggest the most suitable techniques to produce their picture of a fish or plant and, through class discussion and teacher guidance, the four best techniques are agreed upon.

Pupils begin their projects.

Lessons four and five

Pupils work on projects. Teacher hovers and instructs pupils as they come to use their chosen methods.

Lesson six

The work is completed and, as it is done, the teacher marks the work according to her criteria and objectives.

On the other hand, the teacher intending to use an 'experiential' approach might pursue the following:

Lesson one

Pupils are informed that they have six weeks to produce an item to wear or hang on the wall based on the theme 'The Sea'. A box of colourful library books is distributed around the room and pupils are invited to spend a while choosing a picture which they think provides an interesting stimulus. Within twenty minutes pupils are armed with pictures of seagulls, ships of various kinds, plants, fish, sharks, whales, icebergs, jellyfish and so on. Pupils are given the rest of the lesson to produce a simple design based on their picture, to make their item using four of the previous year's techniques.

The teacher spends time discussing individually with pupils the suitability of their pictures, their complexity, what sort of item the design might lend itself to and, at appropriate times, reminding groups of pupils what techniques are available to them. The individual approach is paramount as the diversity of ideas is so great.

Lesson two

Before individual work begins the teacher offers a reminder to the group of what techniques are available and states that pupils have until lesson five to complete the task. The only stipulation now is that pupils check with the teacher before proceeding so that any potential difficulties in production can be discussed and that when techniques are to be used a brief meeting occurs between pupil and teacher so that the teacher is aware that the child knows how to use the technique appropriately and successfully. Appropriate equipment is placed in various work areas around the room.

Lessons three to five

From here until the end of lesson five the teacher offers her services to pupils; helping to decide techniques, considering the pitfalls of the design, analysing the best method to approach the work. All this, done in discussion with pupils individually, helps to synthesise and channel the child's own creative energies. The teacher is also able to monitor, understand and evaluate better the child's thought processes.

Lesson six

A session of evaluation. Pupils are first given the opportunity to consider their own work in the light of the assessments which the teacher wishes to make and, in groups, to discuss the work of each other. Lastly the teacher discusses with each individual the outcome of his or her brief, the problems discovered and so on.

It is not the authors' intention to suggest that one approach is better than the other. Each has its merits. Consider, however, the following questions:

● Is one approach better for overall class control and management?

● Does one approach offer more opportunities for pupils' work to satisfy the aims and objectives of the project?

● Is greater creativity likely to occur in one than in the other?

● Is the teacher's monitoring of achievement likely to be easier or enhanced in one setting or the other?

● What might be the problems and pitfalls of each approach and, therefore, which might be the most acceptable to you?

As a further example of how approaches might vary, consider a Science lesson in which pupils are being taught or discovering how to detect acids and alkalis when presented with several clear, colourless liquids.

Approach one

Pupils in pairs are given a test tube rack with six test tubes containing clear, colourless liquids which are labelled A–F. They are also given litmus paper.
Instructions are as folows:

'You are going to test the liquids in the test tubes to see whether they are acids or alkalis. You have litmus paper in front of you. Dip the litmus paper in each. If it turns red the liquid is acid. If it turns blue the liquid is alkaline. Record the results as follows:

Liquid A turns litmus......
Liquid B turns litmus......
Liquid C turns litmus......
Liquid D turns litmus......
Liquid E turns litmus......
Liquid F turns litmus......

Pupils are then given sodium carbonate, told that it effervesces in acid and, therefore, they can double check results.

'At the end we will discuss your results and check you have the right answers'.

Approach two

Pupils are given the same equipment and also sodium carbonate (which effervesces when dropped into acid).
Instructions are given as follows:

'The test tubes in front of you are labelled A–F but the chemist has muddled them up. You are going to see if you can find out which is which using the litmus paper and sodium carbonate. You must not mix the liquids as that will not help the experiment. I shall give you no more instructions than that at the moment except to say that I want you to find a neat method of recording the results of your experiments'.

Pupils obviously need to know that sodium carbonates causes acids to effervesce but the teacher, feeling that this would detract from the initial 'discoveries', waits until all pupils have experimented and produced results.

He then simply says 'What are your observations?' and records the information on the board. Finally he chooses to tell the pupils that sodium carbonate causes acid to bubble, so asks what further statements pupils can make about the test tubes and the liquids before them. (Alternatively, he could suggest that the following week he will reveal which are acids and alkalis but, in preparation, pupils are to spend homeworks finding out what acids and alkalis do to litmus and sodium carbonate).

Again, to some extent this is a contrived situation but there are two approaches to the same problem. Skill, confidence, experience and knowledge of pupils will help a teacher to decide the most comfortable approach for himself.

As a final thought, consider some of your ideas for the lessons in Practical Task Four. Consider which methods, both didactic and experiential, might be available to you and, theoretically, which might be of greater interest or help to pupils.

In practical terms, classroom management as far as it concerns presentation of material is a complex issue which is influenced by many factors. This chapter has considered such influences in terms of aims and objectives in your subject syllabus, the presentation of the topic, the pupils' needs and teaching methods. Faced with a new class, a new syllabus or a combination of the two most teachers have to work at the presentation of topics to ensure success in the classroom. Redefining ideas, re-presenting work and modification of goals take place often in order that the teacher may manage his/her classroom in its widest sense, successfully. While the experienced teacher might appear to cruise through these problems; the inexperienced can often become dismayed that a re-think is necessary, especially after meticulous preparation. As has already been suggested, don't be afraid to tap someone else's knowledge to help you to see other approaches to your work.

PRACTICAL TASK FOUR

In this exercise you should aim to produce a scheme of work of six fifty minute lessons.

If you are currently teaching in a school, either as a student or teacher, obtain a copy of the school's curricular aims. If you are yet to work in a school, it is feasible to use the suggested aims on page 32. Choose a year group and a topic which you either are, or might be expected to teach as part of your main teaching specialism and which can conceivably be covered in the scheme of work.

Complete the following table, using suitably sized sheets of paper:

A   TOPIC:

B   Theme for each lesson: (head sequential sections as Lesson 1, Lesson 2, Lesson 3, etc.)

C   Briefly outline what are the main objectives for each lesson (skills and knowledge.) (Leave appropriate space to be filled in.)

D   Now, relate these themes and objectives to the overall aims of the department syllabus for the year group and to the school's curricular aims. (Leave appropriate space to be filled in.)

PRACTICAL TASK FIVE

Let us first consider an example of the problems which the teacher might face in presenting a particular topic. In the second week of the term the French teacher has, as a main objective, the teaching of the vocabulary and grammatical structures to enable pupils to greet each other. It is a forty minute lesson, an all-ability, first year class and the pupils have no prior knowledge of the work to be completed. The lesson develops along the following lines (bracketed comments are the teacher's possible thoughts):

Introductory 10 minutes

Teacher concentrates on 'Bonjour, la classe,' to which he anticipates the collective class response, 'Bonjour M. Smith'.

It is hoped that then all pupils individually will say 'Bonjour, la classe' to elicit the response 'Bonjour, Sally or John, etc'.
(I don't wish to give the pupils a direct translation *nor* written words to confuse pronunciation so I anticipate the bright ones will absorb the idea quickly and others follow. Unfortunately, after three minutes, the class are not responding as a group but I'm receiving a jumble of

responses. Answer, perhaps, is to split it into smaller groups so that I have a greater awareness of who is saying what!)

Thus, the plan has changed; the collective class response has been modified to group responses. After a further three minutes, therefore, the teacher is able to switch tactics to pupils speaking to the class as individuals. As this develops he is able to correct individual pupil's pronunciation but also notices that pupils X, Y and Z blush and are unable to respond properly.

(I'll return to these three again in turn but in the meantime I'll try to keep the momentum going by moving others in the group. If I place pupil X after the next two attempts, pupil Y after a further two and pupil Z at the end, they may have grasped the sentence).

Thus, individual need is recognised and, rather than stopping the lesson, allowance is made for further opportunities. Let us assume, however, that even with further opportunities pupils Y and Z are still floundering. Due to the first modification of approach, the teacher is now twelve minutes into the lesson.

(I'll keep my eye on Y and Z, returning to help them later when others are doing pair work.)

Development activities (1) – 15 minutes

The aim is to add 'Ca va?' and elicit the response 'Oui, ca va bien, merci.' Using the same format as before, the teacher greets the class such that the conversation goes:

> 'Bonjour, la classe'.
> 'Bonjour, M. Smith.'
> 'Ca va?'
> Oui, ca va bien, merci.'

(This time the pupils are speaking as a group so I don't need to split them into groups.)

After a minute, the teacher feels that the class have grasped the idea and allows individuals to address the group as in the introductory sequence. This time, however, a few more pupils are floundering.

(I thought this might happen and what I'm most concerned about is that confidence is not lost at such an early stage. I'll move on quickly to the next activity which was planned for the whole class but from which I will now withdraw pupils Y, Z and other strugglers to continue with this exercise with me.)

Again a change of strategy has been required. Only ten minutes of the allocated time for Development Activities has passed.

Development activities (2) – 5 minutes

Pupils are now to wander around the room greeting each other in the above manner. The teacher, however, takes the half dozen strugglers into a corner and does the same exercise more intensively with them. When they are able to do it, he allows them to join the whole class activity, feeling that they have gained in confidence.

Conclusion – 13 minutes are left

Pupils draw two faces, with bubbles coming from mouths where greetings are exchanged. The information has already been written on the board. Several pupils plaintively cry: 'I can't draw, Mr Smith'.

(I've the answer to this one, I'll demonstrate on the board how to draw two right hands, one superimposed on the other in a handshake. Pupils can draw round each others' hands and write the conversation inside.)

The above situation may be rather contrived but it is intended to serve only as an indicator, in a very simple sense, of how lessons need to be modified as they develop.

Consider, now, the lesson objectives you covered in Practical Task Four.

Take one of your lesson themes from that exercise and consider ways in which you might try to develop it as a lesson plan so that the assessment objectives can be met. (If you spend time thinking of several ways to do this, it might help in developing the skills of changing the lesson plan to accommodate different circumstances). Using one of your ideas complete the following table:

Lesson Theme:

Introduction (Time:)

Development (Time:)

Conclusion (Time:)

Now consider the following:

(1) In the middle of the introductory activity, a child arrives late. What contingency plans do you have to facilitate the pupil's easy entry into the group and for him to pick up what he has missed?

(2)   After twenty-five minutes of the lesson, the statemented child whose support teacher is absent bursts into tears, panic stricken that he cannot cope with the work level. How might you deal with this to satisfy the boy's academic and emotional needs which clearly go hand in hand here?

(3)   At the moment before you begin the concluding activities, you notice a child's exercise book, course work exercise, painting (and so on, depending on the type of lesson). Very little work has been done though it is clear that all pupils should have reached the stage which you have envisaged for the end of the lesson. How do you deal with the child? It is too late to recap and staying behind is impossible because it is late autumn, and parents will not allow the child to stay if she must go home in the dark.

(4)   List any other 'sticky' moments, caused by pupils' academic capabilities, which might interrupt your ideas for your lesson. How would you deal with them?

CHAPTER 4

Achieving Academic Potential

What is academic potential?

In Chapter Three we considered the aims and objectives in our teaching when preparing the content and delivery of lessons. The essence of these is clearly to ensure that the 'whole' child is educated in preparation for fitting into the society of which he or she will be part. In the distant past, the 'three Rs', taught in an orderly working atmosphere, were in many ways considered to be sufficient. The Church provided moral or spiritual teaching. This provided a basic education for the majority. As the complexity of society has developed, however, much thought has been given to the role of education in providing a broader basis in preparation for adult life. Hence, subjects like Social or Personal Education have evolved where matters like personal hygiene, sex education, careers, race and gender issues and, more recently, 'green' issues can be considered by pupils. The intention is to raise pupils' awareness of issues relating directly to the society of which they are members and of which they require some understanding.

Despite this, it is still possible to encounter the 'academic education' bandwagon whose members assume that if straightforward academic teaching is not provided for pupils then true education is not taking place. Such attitudes often stem from a longing for a glorious past when pupils learned facts, lists, data and produced them in an examination to show what they had learned and understood. The traditional grammar school was the epitome of this. Such an approach tends to ignore the monitoring of the process by which children learn which plays a part in many G.C.S.E. assessment objectives and is at the heart of much of the National Curriculum.

Thus, it is necessary today to acknowledge the complexity of the teaching, learning and assessment process when defining 'Academic Potential'. Undoubtedly, the fulfilment of potential on the part of every pupil is at the back of every teacher's mind and dictates to some extent the nature of the lesson and the presentation of materials. To suggest that academic implies a more scholarly, conventional approach is no longer sufficient to reflect the developing education process in Great Britain. The following definition, however, should reflect the type of potential we might be considering when analysing just what we wish our pupils to achieve while in our charge.

Academic potential *is* the limit of the acquisition and application of knowledge, of reasoning skills, of creativity and of practical abilities which a pupil is capable of achieving in school.

Such a definition acknowledges the complexity of the learning process, the variety of criteria on which we might assess pupils and the factual knowledge which underpins the whole.

How might it be achieved?

Theoretically, the answer to this question is simple. Devise a means to assess the child's abilities and needs and, once this is complete, set tasks and learning situations which enable the pupil to progress gradually until he or she is able to proceed no further. To survey learning theory and school organisation as they have developed since the 1944 Education Act, however, reveals that it is more difficult than this.

While all schools attempt to provide the best they can for each individual child, the fact that the school is a large institution where buildings, staffing, timetabling and resources dictate to some extent the education process which is provided cannot be ignored. Allied to this, in considering the fulfilment of academic potential, are the philosophical and sociological considerations which also influence pupil groupings, teaching method and school organisation. Since 1944 the tripartite system; the comprehensive system; remedial classes, setting, streaming and all-ability; various teaching methods and the examination system have all been adopted, adapted, altered or rejected in an effort to improve the potential achievement of the pupils. At the same time, language development, home background, sex stereotyping and ethnic background among many other factors have been considered in terms of their influence upon pupil achievement.

Politicians, industrialists, Trades Unionists, Local Government and such groups have all had something to say on the issue. Indeed, the tripartite system and the comprehensive system and the merits of each are deeply entrenched in political philosophy. Such a situation further complicates this desire on a teacher's part simply to help children to achieve their best. Undoubtedly, some aspects of the debate do have political and social implications. For instance, much work has been done on the achievement of pupils from different ethnic backgrounds and it is clear that this is a problem which the teacher in the classroom cannot overcome alone.

Allowing for all the factors inherent in this complex issue which educationalists, politicians, sociologists and psychologists have considered in some detail, let us consider, in a practical way, the teacher in the classroom. For twenty to twenty-five hours each week we are faced with our charges and, while the knowledge of theory, philosophy and past experience will be of great importance, we have to do the best we can to help each child when we may only see him or her for up to three hours a week as a subject teacher and for somewhat less, although in an equally important role when attempting to fulfil potential, as a form tutor.

Thus, day to day, with work to prepare, reports to write, marking, an exam syllabus to follow, registration and pastoral involvement, and the general hectic routine of the school day we must concentrate on the practicalities of pupil achievement.

Assessing potential

Various methods are available to the individual teacher to assess whether the pupils in the classroom are achieving what they are capable of. For the teacher new to the school or new to the class, one of the most important tasks is to ascertain the pupils' abilities and needs as soon as possible. Pupils' written work, discussion work, written exercises, tests set by the individual teacher, standard assessment tests (e.g. reading age tests), practical tasks, examinations and, for a limited number, Statements of Special Educational Needs, provide the means which most teachers employ on a day to day, weekly, termly or yearly basis to assess the needs of their pupils.

The arrival of the National Curriculum formalises the assessments which good teachers have made for many years. Briefly, the introduction of standard attainments targets and the assessment of pupils' attainments in each of the four key stages (Key Stage 1: Years

1-2, 5-7 year olds; Key Stage 2: Years 3-6, 7-11 year olds; Key Stage 3: Years 7-9, 11-14 year olds; Key Stage 4: Years 10-11, 14-16 year olds) will ensure that a pupil's achievement is measured against common standards, using common criteria with a view to giving a formal account of what a pupil has achieved and where help might be needed in the future. The National Curriculum makes it specifically clear how assessments will ensure that we, as teachers, are able to gain a clear indication of this. It is stated that assessments should be (a) 'formative' in that they should give need to develop to the next stage; (b) 'summative' in showing what a pupil has achieved.

Informally, however, the monitoring of a pupil's work on a lesson by lesson basis is the way in which teachers generally consider what is being achieved and where help is needed.

Let us assume that a piece of English work has been set for a group of mixed-ability youngsters in a first year class. The task is to write a narrative piece in which the youngsters have to write about their experiences of missing a stop on the train or bus, or going in the wrong direction because they misheard a platform announcement and find themselves in a strange place with no money and no means to get home. This is a follow up to an extract from the story *Emil and the Detectives* by Erich Kastner.

CLASSWORK (1)   *Kelly*
The Journey

I can't wate i'm going to my cousins house, so there you can't go. Now stop that Kelly otherwise you won't go either. your brother would go its just that he's not old enogh yet, but he will be going with you next year. I want to go! look said mum we will go to Alton Towers instead. Now Kelly go and pack your things for going to your anties house. Mum I want to ask you somthing. What? can I go to the station on my own, please, please, please. No you can certanly not go on your own anything could happen to you. But mum. No and thats it, end of subject. I'm going to pack my things, and don't bother with lunch I won't be hungry. Kelly! What! come down stairs. What are you doing you have been in your room for 3 hours its time for bed now. Kelly hurry up and get up your going to your anuties house ok! Mum I don't want my breakfast I'm not hungry. DaD can I go to the station on my own! I don't mind, but you will have to ask you mum first. Mum can I go to the station on my own. no you can not, I'v already told you. OK. come on lets go. mum! yes. can you just drop me off at the station and I will get the ticket and everything. yes! Ok! thanks mum. Bye dad Bye Paul Bye Mum. Don't worry I'v got my ticket I'll get the right train don't worry. now mum said get on platform 2 so wheres 2 o'h it's there. Now I will have to wait for the train to come. o'h its here now, make shore its the right one. Yes! now I have to get of at Belper. so thats a few stops away. Now what can I do. I now I shall read my comic smash hits. I'm board I will listen to my stero instead. Theres nothing on there either. I am pretty tierd I think I will have a nap now, its not my stop for a very long time. Whats that! Hey why are you pushing me! Sorry, but your the last on the train and I wonder what stop you wanted. Er, er I wanted Belper please. O'h sorry but we went past Belper an hour ago. O'h well I will try the phone thankyou bye. Now I'm sure I've got some money in my bag. Right 10p let me phone up: 798510 Its' not ringing whats happend. O'h no its not working, so now what am I going to do. I know I will write to them Lets get my things out. Dear . . . , I don't belive this my pens ran out. I will just go and waite in the car park. Next day. I hope I see a friend so she can take me home. Hey lucy! Hi Kelly. What are you doing here. Well its a long story I'll tell you later. Were are you going. We have just come back from our holiday and were going home now. Shall I ask you mum if I can come with you. Ok. Mrs Shorecroft can I ask you something? Please may I come home with you because I am meant to being going to may Aunties house but I missed my stop. Yes dear of course you can come with us. come on this is our car now tell me what this is all about. O'h I will tell you when we get to my house. As I have told you Its a long story. Right here we are. Hi mum! I can explain. Why don't you stay for tea lucy? And then I will tell your family and my family what this is all about!

CLASSWORK (2)   *Tracey*
My Mistake

I was on my way to the station, I am going to my Auntie's for the day. We got out of the taxi. my mum, told the driver to wait because she was getting back in after she had nagged at me about everything she could think of and then it would cost her about £10 pounds. She told me to "be polite", Clean-up for her, made sure I had some money for dinner, made sure I had somethink to drink, and remember your HONK! manners. My mum started to scream and shout at him because he was being rude. it was so embarrasing I must of been as red as a tomato. I couldn't wait any longer I told my mum my train left in 10 mins she kissed me good-bye and hugged me and repeated what she had allready told me and got in the taxi and drove off nagging to the taxi driver. I ran to the ticket office and got a ticket for a return day to Belper. the train left in 3 mins on platform 2. I ran to platform 2 and jumped on the train and it started moving. The speaker said the train on platform 2 is leaving in 10 mins. it stops at Leeds, Belper "BELPER"! Excuse me sir, "Is this train leaving for Belper?" "No this is going to Liverpool and then "Oh NO!" I jumped out of my seat and ran down the train but the train was already moving so I wnet back to my seat and sat down and started to think what I was going to do. I was getting all panicy and I was sweating. I got ready to get of the next stop it was Leeds. I got of the train and sat in a seat I was there for ages then suddenly a man came up to me. he was a train driver. He asked me where I was going." "I said "I don't really know but I'm trying to get to Belper to my auntie's" The man said "well the nest train is in 10 minutes" I said "I haven't any money" The man sat there thinking. I looked at him he had dark brown hair a big pimple on his nose. He suddenly jumped in the air "I know, if I give you the fair to get there you come back and give me the money back tomorrow" I said "Okay" I got on the next train to Belper and when I got to my auntie's I told her what had happened. I phoned my mum and told her I was staying at aunties for a few more days. I was on my way home, I never did give that train driver his money back. I bet he's still waiting there now. When I got home I told my mum about my mistake and about what happened to the train driver. she just laughed. I don't think i'll be going on a train again untill I'm over my mistake.

Methods of assessment

There are various ways in which the above work can be assessed. Children always like to be aware of whether their work is improving and, if so, how. A basic criterion for assessment, therefore, is to examine these pieces of work against work that has been done previously. If, for example, the pupil is showing that he or she is beginning to employ a wider variety of sentence structures, this might be worthy of praise or, on the other hand, if he or she is clearly not writing in sufficient detail on this occasion but does do so usually, a reminder to examine this essay at the side of another piece of sufficiently detailed work might be valid. In this way, a pupil should be seeing some development in his or her work in a simple, but useful, way.

The variety of potential assessments of the above work, however, are numerous. It might be assessed:

(1) *On content*
    – is it relevant to the title?
    – does the story develop in an interesting way?
    – are the characters credible?
    – does the story make sense?
    and so on . . .

(2) *On style*
    – does the child choose an appropriate style for the task in hand?
    – is the sentence structure suitable?
    – if the story is meant to be amusing does the style reflect this?
    and so on . . .

(3) *On punctuation*
- is the use of capital letters and full stops correct?
  (if not, is there a pattern which can be identified and with which the child can be helped?)
- are commas used correctly?
- if direct speech is used, is it both accurate and relevant and is it clear who is speaking?

(4) *On organisation*
- is the story chronological?
  (if not, does the child still sequence the story to make sense?)
- is it well paragraphed?
- does the story have a beginning, a middle and an end?

The list of potential assessment criteria makes it quite clear that the teacher, when assessing the child's potential and his or her needs, must be clear about what is being assessed; about the criteria against which the work is being assessed and, above all, ensure that consistency is maintained.

Having decided what major criteria the child's work is being assessed against, it is necessary to develop a mark scheme to reflect this and which will produce final marks, grades or comments in order to offer realistic appraisal of the child's development so far and also to encourage the child to develop his or her potential further.

Let us assume, therefore, that the teacher is marking the two extracts above. He is aware that to compare one with the other would be unfair as it is clear that one is more able than the other. At the end of the last piece of work, however, he had decided to talk about capital letters and full stops as many pupils were making basic mistakes in this area. Before this piece of work, he had talked about remembering to ensure that the work is legible and about ensuring that the story had a moment of tension or climax in it. (Discussion had taken place about films, soap operas and series on the television where the plots had been contrived to ensure that interest is maintained by creating many moments of tension, for example).

The teacher decides, therefore, that these three areas are to form the basis of his assessment. Pupils have been made aware of this and the teacher then prepares a mark scheme based on this. Thus he might put the following at the bottom of piece number one:

> Make the difference between your capital letters much clearer. It is also difficult to tell exactly who is speaking at times – see me about this. Good, clear writing but try to plan your work more carefully before writing, in order to build to a climax.

At the bottom of piece number two he might write the following:

> A good attempt at creating the feelings of worry and panic at being on the wrong train and the relief and guilt of being offered the money to go home. Keep working at developing these climaxes of feeling. Clearly written and you use capital letters and full stops very well, on the whole.

Thus, each piece of work has been assessed against criteria which the teacher has formulated and against the pupil's past performance. The remarks are intended to offer a realistic appraisal but also offer encouragement to fulfil potential.

It is often found that work is marked with 'B + Good' or some such comment. In many ways this is worthless as it stands. If, however, a teacher is able to suggest to pupils what value is placed on each grade in a grading system, such comments do have validity. Many teachers would suggest that there is not time to write full comments on all work. This is often true. Two factors stressed so far, however, and of paramount importance when marking work if we are to help pupils to fulfil their academic potential are:

- worthwhile, clearly stated criteria;
- consistency and encouragement which should be inherent in the marking system.

While there are times when we are under pressure and marking is hurried, all pupils should have some of their work assessed carefully on a regular basis.

For the novice teacher, faced with twenty-five or thirty different pieces of work, all of different standards, the feeling of 'where to start?' is not unnatural. There may be a common marking policy in the department or certain 'unwritten rules' such as not correcting too much work in order not to discourage people. Such systems should be adopted quickly but it is often the case that, as with your relationship with the class you teach, a flexible manner and a desire to find an approach which works in your circumstances is of most importance.

As already stated, there are innumerable ways to identify the 'academic potential' of children in the classroom.

Some informal methods

More and more, interaction with pupils on a one-to-one or group basis is being encouraged in schools. Discussion with pupils has one distinct advantage over a piece of written work; while the written work is the end product of the child's thought processes, discussion work allows the teacher to understand these processes as the child ruminates over a problem. Hence, for a pupil to be given a problem to be solved in Maths, for example, and then be offered the opportunity to explain how he or she might work through it, can highlight how the child perceives the questions and reveal any flaws in his or her thinking. Another distinct advantage of this approach is that you are not considering a child's work with her possibly several days after the task has been completed; instead, her mind is concentrating on that problem at that particular moment and, therefore, any monitoring or evaluation which you might offer is of immediate relevance.

Of course, not all learning situations will lend themselves to this kind of approach and, if pupils feel that they are being 'marked' in this situation rather than simply discussing a problem with the teacher, the thinking can be inhibited. Of greatest importance to the probationary or inexperienced teacher, however, are the organisational difficulties which work of this nature might bring. To deal with one individual or small group for several minutes necessitates others working alone without the teacher monitoring behaviour or work rate. Many young teachers find this a daunting prospect. It is a natural desire to want total control of all that is going on at any one time. Assessing potential through discussion, therefore, demands confidence and good classroom relationships. To reach this position may mean that you do not adopt such an approach unless it is required by the syllabus, until you feel happy with the class, their work and your ability to keep everyone gainfully and relevantly occupied.

Do not underestimate discussion work as a vehicle for assessing potential, however. It can, in the appropriate circumstances, enhance your standing and relationships with a class. As with so much of the education process, if your pupils, the consumers, are aware of what and why something is being done they will accept the situation more readily. Again, clearly specified criteria for assessment and positive feedback must provide the basis for this work and it can, because it draws pupil and teacher together, be the most rewarding approach of all!

Structured assessment exercises

Far more easily handled in the classroom situation are exercises to assess potential. Structured questions which demand that pupils reveal their understanding of a topic can be helpful in a diagnostic sense and offer the teacher an opportunity to consider the ability of the pupils, their speed of work, areas of weakness, areas of strength and the needs of the pupils for the future. Of greatest importance when employing this method, however, is the structuring of questions. It is undoubtedly true that anyone can set twenty comprehension questions, a few Maths questions, a set of questions on a history topic but, if such work is to be of any value to pupil and teacher, they need to be carefully compiled.

Consider the following exercise as an example of this:

The Accident

Read the following accounts of the same road accident involving a driver and a 12 year old girl who suffered a broken leg and bruising.

A *Driver*:   I was driving down the street, overtaking a line of three cars and an ice-cream van. At the time I was indicating that I would turn left at the 'T' junction at the bottom of the street which was approximately 30 yards beyond the front of the ice-cream van. My speed was approximately 25 miles per hour when suddenly, from between the ice-cream van and the car behind it, the child ran in front of me without looking. I could not avoid running her over.

B *12 year old child*:   My mates stood on the opposite side of the road while I went to buy an ice-cream. I had already crossed the road in front of the ice-cream van. I bought my ice-cream, walked to the back of the van, looked, listened, and crossed. When I started to cross I could not see the car. It appeared from nowhere; it was going very fast. I could not move out of the way before he hit me.

C *Evidence of one of the girl's friends*:   We were on the other side of the road when Sally, that's my friend who was knocked down, went to buy an ice-cream. She came back through the gap between the ice-cream van and the car behind it. She looked, I think, started to cross the road and suddenly this car appeared from nowhere. He must have been going 60 or more. He never stopped. Sally never had a chance. It was terrible.

D *Evidence of a woman on the 'T' junction who claimed to see everything that happened*:   I was walking home from the supermarket and I saw it all. First, the girl came out at the front of the car, behind the ice-cream van. She looked down the road towards me and then began to cross. She did not seem to notice the car coming down the road towards her. The driver swerved to miss her but could not avoid hitting her, even though he braked hard. I think he must have been doing about 45 miles an hour. After that we all waited for the police and ambulance.

Your task:

(1) Construct a diagram of the accident, with the positions of the girl, the cars, observers and road layout included.
(2) Write a report of the accident using the above information, including an analysis of who was to blame with full justification of your views.
(3) Write on one of the following topics:
   (a) The world is not as safe as it used to be.
   (b) "Accidents will happen".
   (c) The most dangerous moment in my life.

Tasks, tests and examinations

Standard Assessment Tasks are destined to become a feature of the National Curriculum. Their advantage is that pupils' scores give some indication of how they compare with other pupils on an average. They are often diagnostic tests, too. Many reading tests, for example, offer an indication of a pupil's reading age and whether there are any specific difficulties with phonic blends for example. While such tests may become a feature of all subjects as the National Curriculum machinery begins to work, there are presently a limited number of such tests which are only relevant to a few subjects.

Examinations still command most respect in the eyes of the public as indicators of a child's academic potential. The final G.C.S.E. examination grades are often considered by employers as the determiners of whether a youngster is suitable for the type of work which they might need to do. Such an approach is understandably valid to a member of the public but such exams are of little value to the classroom teacher as they are taken at the end of a course. Of course, as pupils complete more and more coursework towards G.C.S.E. examinations the teacher is able to be a little more diagnostic in his or her approach to helping the child.

Examinations completed internally (i.e. for the sake of the class teacher and the pupil) can be of value, however. At the end of a unit of work, of a half term and so on the teacher is able to obtain a good idea of what a pupil has achieved both in knowledge and skills. Once again, such exams should not be simply a test but designed to aid teacher and pupil in defining future goals. Such examinations can reveal aspects of a child's development which might be unclear under other types of assessment. The ability to work at speed, to work without help; to manage time; to apply previously learned knowledge and skills; to memorise and learn are factors common to all examinations.

Practical tasks, whether they be Chemistry experiments, Geography simulations or Home Economics investigations, are increasing in number as a way to assess pupil development. As with oral work which we considered earlier, for the inexperienced teacher the physical organisation and overall classroom control are the factors which might cause most concern. Nonetheless, they are accepted as valid methods of pupil assessment and must be done. Thorough preparation of materials, a clear idea of how the session is to develop and, as far as you are able, only assessing manageable numbers at one time in order to do justice to all is the best way to ensure success. As with assessment through discussion it is a demanding approach but also highly rewarding when successful. If things go wrong and you feel that pupils have not reflected what they are capable of in the work which they have done, it is necessary to consider why not. Analyse the problems as objectively as possible, employ the help of the Head of Faculty or Department and attempt to find a better method for future reference.

We have considered above the different methods to assess pupils' progress and potential which an inexperienced teacher might be called upon to employ. Each has its place and some are probably of greater relevance to your situation than others. When considering assessment of work, however, key stages can clearly be identified:

(1) Define your criteria for assessment.
(2) Devise an appropriate assessment exercise or programme, considering both content and type of assessment.
(3) In preparing a mark scheme, bear in mind both your assessment criteria and diagnosis of pupil potential.
(4) Ensure that pupils receive clear indication of this diagnosis.
(5) Use this information as a stepping stone towards the next stage in your and your pupils' work.

Now consider Practical Test Six at the end of the chapter.

Other indicators of under-achievement

While steps 1–5 above, suggest a straightforward route to the goal of improving pupil performance, it is necessary for the inexperienced teacher to understand that many factors, besides the teacher's own formal and informal assessments, might indicate the degree to which a child is either failing or, of equal validity, is being failed because the work which is set is not demanding enough. Many of these factors might manifest themselves in a pupil's behaviour. She or he might begin to develop undesirable behaviour patterns in certain class-room situations for reasons which are closely related to the pupil's work.

Take, for example, the following case. Sally has had problems throughout secondary school both socially and academically. Indeed, her problems with peers have occurred because they taunt her over her inability to read properly or work at the pace of the majority of pupils in the class. She has always received support in some lessons where such help is both deemed appropriate and available, and has also been withdrawn, during the first three years of secondary schooling, for extra English lessons. Clearly a low achiever, she has required, and responded well to, careful sensitive support and help from classroom teachers. By the middle of the fourth year, however, she is exhibiting very difficult behaviour spasmodically in some lessons. Initially, her form tutor and year tutor have tried to counsel her, spoken to her parents, supported staff who have ensured that Sally is disciplined for misdemeanours. Little is changing, however, but a clear pattern is beginning to emerge. Formal assessment is now taking place as part of examination work and it is under such circumstances, when Sally is expected to work independently and at a pace which she finds uncomfortable, that she demonstrates a stubborn attitude, rudeness to staff and an unwillingness to bring appropriate equipment to the lesson.

Sally clearly feels that she is not achieving that which she is capable of and that the support and help she obviously needs is being withheld. Consequently, a situation develops where Sally's lack of achievement is indicated not only by the work which she produces but by her behaviour too.

Thus, the achievement of academic potential might reveal itself not only in the fulfilling of assessment criteria which the teacher chooses but may also appear in the overall classroom atmosphere and behaviour, which, in turn, calls upon the individual teacher's skills in managing the class socially as well as academically and formulating judgements on achievement as a consequence.

While each child may manifest his or her lack of achievement in an individual, subtle way, there are certain behaviours which may occur and which may be grouped as follows:

(1)   Boredom; vagueness; dreaming; inattentiveness.
(2)   Inability to complete work in a satisfactory way; for instance, refusing to do homework, failing to bring equipment.
(3)   'Stalling' tactics; upset or tearful behaviour; petty quibbles about work or other people; lateness to lessons; attempting to organise or influence the seating arrangements in the classroom; creating 'diversions' from the task in hand.
(4)   Completing work early, without due care; too quickly; of a standard which has deteriorated compared with past work.
(5)   Truancy from the class; from school (possibly with parental collaboration); excuses to leave the class (and possibly being out of the room longer than necessary).

While the above list is not exhaustive it covers most of the obvious ways in which a pupil's inability to achieve might manifest itself behaviourally. There are obviously many other reasons why pupils might employ these 'tactics' in your classroom. The task on your part is to analyse these behaviours and relate them to the pupil's general standard of work to see the likely reasons for such an attitude.

There may, of course, be many other reasons for poor behaviour by pupils and these are dealt with elsewhere in this book. It may be that something outside your classroom, a problem at home or an incident which occurred at break or in the last lesson is the cause. As a starting point, a discussion with the pupil as to the basis of the difficulty might be fruitful. In a class of sensitive adolescents it is highly unlikely that any information is to be forthcoming if you offer to discuss the matter within the hearing of others. Outside the classroom door, after the lesson or in a part of the room where a private conversation can take place would provide a suitable opportunity for discussion. Be sure of the way you see the difficulty but invite the child to consider his or her problems in a non-threatening way in the first instance. To suggest, for example, that you have noticed the pupil is completing work very early, untidily and with many careless errors which did not happen x weeks ago might be the key to opening up the issue, if the pupil is then given the opportunity to explain. In a good relationship the pupil might immediately state that the work is too difficult or too easy and progress can be made. There is also a very strong possibility that no such information will be immediately forthcoming and prying more deeply might provide the answer.

Our view, throughout this book, is that the inexperienced teacher is often faced with problems which appear daunting but which with experience, advice or practical help, can be often resolved without too much stress. The example above is one in which confidence in dealing with youngsters when attempting to diagnose problems with work is paramount. If you feel unsure, the form tutor is probably best able to help. He or she will probably be aware if this is a common problem with this child and advise you accordingly, or may be able to offer background detail or advice which might help in dealing with the child.

If, of course, the pupil is unwilling to discuss the difficulty or take advice and there appears to be no apparent background reason for his or her behaviour, the situation should be dealt with as a simple disciplinary matter by following the agreed code of practice current in your school.

Let us assume, however, that the problem is caused by a difficulty over work. How should you deal with it?

Solutions and strategies

In the first instance, the pupil has told you that the work is too easy, he is bored; there is no interest for him in the current work, and it is, therefore, irrelevant. Whether this is said to you as directly as this, more subtly or via a third party, it can be a severe dent in the self-esteem of the inexperienced teacher. There is little doubt that you are being challenged! As the provider of the learning experience, there is no doubt that it is incumbent upon you to change the situation. In order to retain your confidence and self-esteem, it is often a good ploy to throw the challenge back. If the youngster is not completing tasks it is a perfectly legitimate approach to point this out and make it clear that if your work is too easy you would anticipate that it would be completed properly and carefully. The child would then have a justifiable complaint. Such approaches usually dampen the spirit of the individual who is merely citing easy work as a vehicle for disruptive behaviour.

On the other hand, the child who tells you the same thing but is completing the work which you set in a satisfactory manner is providing a different but quite legitimate problem. In this circumstance, the teacher is failing the child and is not providing opportunities for the child to fulfil her or his potential. In such circumstances the following needs to be considered:

- Is the child's understanding such that he or she can handle extension work without completing further work of this type?
- Will the child miss anything vital in the curriculum or which is relevant to assessments if he or she is provided with something else?

If the answer to the first is 'yes' and to the second 'no', then it is incumbent upon the teacher to provide further work of a type which the pupil is to be interested in and extended by. The trap to avoid is setting something difficult or too demanding for the sake of it.

The same situation applies, of course, if the whole class complains of the same thing. If a class legitimately makes it clear that the work is too easy, you have obviously miscalculated their ability. In such circumstances, it may be that the work needs to be completed to cover the appropriate aspect of the syllabus but this could be done quickly in order to provide more demanding work. Alternatively, if the need to cover the syllabus does not arise, re-think your course either beginning something new or approaching your current work in a way which is more demanding through what it expects of your pupils.

At the opposite extreme, the pupils who are providing problems because the work is too difficult often appear in greater numbers. This is probably because it is easier for the teacher to spot the problem in a more tangible way; incomplete classwork, half-finished exercises, tearful behaviour when work is set, trying to be the class clown rather than work at all. Based on the assumption that it has been made clear to you that the reason for a pupil's difficulties in your classroom is because he or she cannot do the work, it is necessary to analyse the individual's work patterns and possible solutions. Such questions are:

- Are there particular skills which he or she cannot master and which I can help him or her to overcome during the lesson, at the end or after school?
- Is this a part of curriculum which all pupils have to master before the next stage and, therefore, he or she must understand?
- Is it necessary, for this individual, because of his or her ability, to have an individual work programme rather than follow the work of the majority? (Think of the social consequences for Sally in this situation!)
- Would it be appropriate to ask for help from a support teacher for a couple of lessons to help him or her overcome the problem?

Pupils can often be delighted (and sometimes surprised!) that such solutions are available rather than continuing to be frustrated and behaving accordingly. Your esteem in his or her eyes is, we would suggest, bound to increase by being so sensitive to the difficulties rather than simply attempting to quell the inappropriate behaviour! (That is not to deny, of course, that sometimes formally imposed discipline is the most appropriate method to deal with poor pupil behaviour).

As with other problems, do seek help. If, for instance, you attempt to resolve the problem within the classroom but without success, approach your Head of Department. It might be that a move to a different class, either for social or academic reasons (if classes are setted or streamed for example) might be in the best interests of the pupil.

Thus far, we have considered behavioural traits which might indicate that a child is not achieving but there are many other inimical factors which might influence a pupil's potential and which it may be more difficult for you to do something about.

Health problems

A pupil in your class may unfortunately be suffering from various health problems which influence attendance, concentration, ability to complete work and ultimately, therefore, achievement. Such factors may be particularly painful periods for a girl which force her to be confined to bed for a day or so on a regular basis. Hay fever and asthma are further examples of the types of 'illness' which can cause absence and consequently stress for the pupil who realises that he or she is falling behind with work.

In such circumstances, it is necessary for the teacher to be as sensitive and supportive as possible of the pupil. It is very easy to berate a pupil for failing to complete work, to point out that she or he is falling behind and that regular attendance is causing concern when the pupil is already aware of this and is very anxious. A word with a form teacher if, for example, regular inattendance is occurring may provide you with information which helps you to see the problem from a different perspective. A sensitive approach might be to allow the pupils to explain why the illness causes problems and how, in partnership, you can ensure that the work is done, even if this means allowing a pupil extra time in which to complete it. When a pupil has been absent for some time a similar approach might apply. If his lack of understanding is because of absence earlier in the course and missing pieces of key knowledge then it may be necessary to provide an individual work programme.

Other common health problems which might well not come to your attention unless you have been given prior knowledge through the pastoral welfare system of the school are hearing and sight defects. Sensitive and emotional youngsters who wish to be seen as 'normal' by their peers might make every effort possible to avoid letting the problem show. It is not infrequent to find that the fifteen year old whose handwriting is appalling and who either squints at the chalkboard or seems to need his partner's attention whenever he or she wishes to take information from it should have been wearing glasses for the last six months!

Once again, sensitive handling of the situation is of paramount importance and a quiet word offering help such as sitting nearer the board or sitting to your left if the pupil has a hearing problem in his right ear might be sufficient. It can be argued that the teacher who discovers that a pupil in his class who has sat at the back and struggled for months and should be wearing glasses but who approaches it by shouting across the class – 'And I know you should be wearing glasses, I thought there was something wrong. Why don't you wear them when there is nothing to be ashamed of?' – deserves every potential discipline problem he or she might get! (A tell-tale sign of a hearing defect can often be seen when a pupil turns his or her head to a certain angle when listening to you).

Social factors

Many social factors can influence achievement and to deal with them adequately would require another volume. However, the classroom teacher needs to be aware of the types of social factors which play a part in a pupil's achievement.

A child's relationship with peers is of, perhaps, the greatest influence in this area. He or she may be involved with a group outside the classroom who expect him or her to set certain behavioural or attitudinal standards inside it. Alternatively, a pupil may be seeking credibility with other pupils and therefore take on traits which do not reflect true ability. The child may be the victim of bullying or victimisation which does not manifest itself openly in the classroom but subtly ensures that his or her concentration is not on work but on the pressures which others cause. Role models who influence youth culture can be the greatest source of motivation or demotivation for pupils. A few years ago, one of the authors was confronted by a pupil at the end of a lesson who suggested that there was no reason to work at school because he had heard person X (a female recording artist who had some success in the early eighties and who subsequently became an actress) state that she had not worked at school, achieved very little by way of exam qualifications which subsequently proved worthless to her, but was doing very nicely thank you. Such attitudes can often distort a child's view and there is a need to explore individually the notion of success and achievement (and in this case, the possibility of making records successfully!)

The chief problem when considering the sociometry of the classroom is that the influences on a child's work are not always obvious and the teacher needs to be ever vigilant about the ways in which the dynamic friendships are changing and whether this is influencing work patterns. Where there is obvious influence, however, solutions are relatively easy; moving pupils, ensuring that the withdrawn child who is not working through a lack of self-esteem in the group plays a major role in group work and so on.

The influence on attitude and achievement which is possibly of greatest significance socially but which it is the most difficult to do something about is that of the family. If a pupil is offered negative attitudes at home about the importance of school and work it becomes difficult for him or her to see any intrinsic value in it. Consequently, achievement is limited. Undue and unfair pressures on a child at home can simply aggravate any problems he or she may be having with school work. Examples such as having to look after younger children in the evening while mother and father work; having to prepare meals; getting younger siblings ready for school at an early hour while mother and father go to work; sharing a bedroom; no quiet place in the house to work; stresses in the marital relationship which are being foisted upon children are known to harm children's potential achievement. Such circumstances are not really the realm of the inexperienced teacher to resolve, although the child in this situation often seeks out a teacher whom he or she feels able to trust in order to talk the situation through and relieve some of the tensions. If information is forthcoming to you which worries you or if you wish to ascertain whether there might be problems of which you are unaware, the year tutor or form tutor is often a source of information or, on the other hand, is in a position to perhaps approach the family expressing your concerns.

The importance of language

Earlier in this chapter, the problems of a girl called Sally were mentioned and they exemplify what can be one of the chief factors in a child's achievement: language. Much work, from Basil Bernstein onwards, has been produced to show that language development and academic ability are interlinked. In the classroom setting, however, the readability of articles, questions, or instructions are often of paramount importance to a child's ability to complete work satisfactorily. The child who experiences few problems with mathematical concepts but whose achievement is limited by an inability to overcome the language of the questions is not uncommon. It is very easy to set questions or present material which the inexperienced teacher feels is appropriate but where the language of the piece is couched in 'adult' terms rather than in a style which younger pupils find accessible. The problem for the inexperienced teacher is having to work at the pupils' level after pursuing his or her own academic career to a high level. This also applies to oral instructions. The teacher who says to a class of twelve year olds in a Personal and Social Education lesson on study skills – 'I would like you to reflect on and analyse your current work practices with a view to improving the effectiveness of your learning' – is clearly going to experience difficulties in teaching his charges.

Always be aware of your use of language, the readability of your work and be prepared to change or modify what you are presenting so that, in fairness to all, the opportunity for the pupils to achieve their potential is not hindered.

Conclusions

We began this chapter with a working definition of academic potential and subsequently considered how it might be assessed and how we might be restricting achievement. Our intention has been to raise the inexperienced teacher's awareness of the complexity of the problem and to proffer relatively simple solutions which he or she might feel comfortable with when setting out on a career in teaching.

The basic tenet, at the beginning, was that if we are aware of current achievements by pupils, then we are in a position to ensure further success and the fulfilment of potential. By being aware of a child's current stage of development and the various other factors which might influence achievement, we are in a position to provide suitable work. We should be able to produce lessons where the content, its delivery, in terms of pace, teaching, style and learning experience are of a type which enhances the child's progress. In diagrammatic terms, the process of achievement on a day-to-day basis in school might be seen as in Figure 1. The preparation of this work and the teaching and learning experience will be considered in the next chapter.

Figure 1.

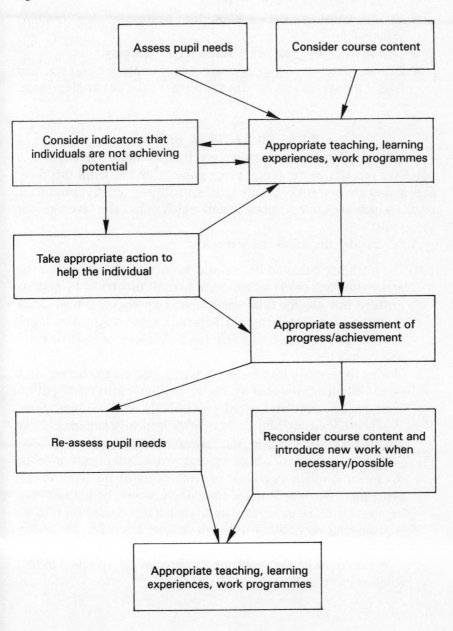

PRACTICAL TASK SIX

Consider one element of the syllabus for a lower school class in your subject which you have been selected to teach either on teaching practice or in your first year of teaching.

● Decide what it is you are to teach.
● Briefly consider the method of delivering this teaching experience.
● Decide next how you will assess a pupil's success.
● Devise, therefore, an appropriate means of assessment; consider both your assessment criteria and a mark scheme to reflect these.

PRACTICAL TASK SEVEN

Steven is a pupil in your year eight class. It is the end of November and you have recently begun a new programme of work. Until this time, Steven had always worked quite satisfactorily and quietly, producing results which are quite acceptable and which reflect the 'average' for the group.

Now consider the following scenarios:

(1) His work has begun to deteriorate; homeworks are not done; he arrives late and draws attention to himself on arrival by making profuse but clearly false excuses and apologies. From being 'average', his standards are slipping. How might you work towards helping him back to his acceptable level of work rate and achievement?

(2) During the last two lessons Steven has sat and completed no work at all. When approached by you he has burst into tears, put his head on his arms and asked you politely to leave him alone. Pupils are ignoring him and his work is clearly suffering. How might you help? Consider the various alternatives.

(3) Steven is happy to complete oral work, take part in class discussion and shows a clear understanding of the work in this programe. When he is asked to write, however, he has begun to say that he has no equipment and, when it is provided for him, he is producing very untidy work which does not reflect the ability which he has shown in the past.

What might be the problems and how might you help to find solutions to them?

While there might be many reasons for the above behaviour patterns and experience will help you to ascertain their cause and how to overcome them, for the purpose of this exercise, assume that your sole consideration is ensuring that Steven fulfils his academic potential in that programme of work and that other factors are secondary.

CHAPTER 5

Administrative Necessities

Amongst the many tasks you will be expected to undertake, often without any prior experience, are the time consuming and, often onerous, duties of:

- Record keeping (mark books and attendance)
- Marking work and relevance of comments
- Report writing
- Making referrals (see also Chapter Six)

Many schools will have different policies on the above, some will have no obvious policy, but all to a greater or lesser extent will expect you to undertake them in some form. All the procedures are useful to you as a practising teacher anyway, and the Education Act (1988) has enshrined them in law as part of the teacher's professional duties, so establishing a working procedure at an early stage would be an advantage to you.

Record keeping

All schools will supply you with some form of record/mark book – it may be an A4 squared paper type or a loose leaf format; to make the best use of it, divide it into sections, say several pages for each group which has been assigned to you. In planning your lessons, try to keep at least one or two ahead of the one you are actually teaching and make a one or two line summary of your intentions for that lesson, leaving a space for comment beneath, after completion of the session. An example for an English lesson might read like this:

> Read poem to the class. Split class into groups for discussion. Ask whole class as a result to make rough notes in preparation for essay next lesson, working individually.

Comment (added later):

> Class needs more practice at group work. Concentrate on this next week.

However, ideas even if ideal on paper do not always work well in practice, owing to group chemistry, the weather or any other factor. You will be surprised how much difference a windy day, the first snow of winter or heavy rain will make to the behaviour of your classes! Always have a 'standby' idea that you can use if you sense that the time is not right for your planned idea.

It is always a good idea to have an accurate alphabetical list of pupils' names in your mark book at the beginning of the section dedicated to that group. When first taking over a group with which you are not familiar, draw a seating plan and ask pupils to sit in the same places for a few weeks until you know their names. Keeping your mark book with the seating plan surreptitiously open on your desk will aid your confidence, speed your memory with regard to names and give you more immediate authority over your group.

Keep a record of attendance for each lesson. This is in addition to the normal attendance registers which, if assigned a tutor group, you will be required to keep. By doing this you will know immediately which pupil was absent on a particular day, pinpointing accurately which work has been missed. This is vital with the current importance of continuous assessment in year ten upwards.

Some schools may require you to register pupils for each lesson anyway as a precaution against truancy and maintaining your own records will make this easier.

Marking work

When you set a piece of written work, your pupils and their parents will expect you to mark it; there is always a temptation to set work in order that you can concentrate on an individual or a small group within the class whilst the others are working. The resulting work will add to your marking load. This 'marking load', is one of the major causes of fatigue in the first year of teaching and you should try to 'pace' yourself accordingly. Strictly speaking, you should avoid setting work that doesn't require marking, but it sometimes expedites matters to do so! If you do, clearly explain to your pupils that it is 'rough notes' only for a future, more formal, piece of writing, or, quite simply, that you do not intend to mark it anyway. Honesty of this kind is often preferable to raising pupil expectations and consequent parental ire: use it sparingly however.

On occasions when you do mark a piece of work, do not become laboured. Some subjects may be marked 'over the shoulder' of a pupil during a lesson where everyone is working quietly, others may require more detailed analysis. When this is the case, read through it quickly noting any obvious spelling errors, annotating the correct spelling in the margin nearby. *Never* just tick a piece of work, write a simple summative comment at the end of the final paragraph, always ending on a positive note if you can. For example, you may wish to point out some error whilst praising the imaginative or accurate content or style, or indeed the level of effort required to produce the work. Always remember the key word – *motivation*. All pupils will (even if it is not immediately obvious), flourish with praise over a period of time. If you are using a mark scheme always add a comment to the mark. It may be obvious, but it is worth remembering that a child who produces work of a poor technical standard may have exerted tremendous effort to do so. *Reward that effort*. Equally a more able pupil may have produced something eminently acceptable, but of a standard below his or her potential: register your cognisance of this fact.

In conclusion, make your comments 'two pronged'; locate and comment upon areas of weakness, but counter this by searching for something to praise and give the student an avenue of escape along which he may develop to improve his standard.

Report writing

Reports have developed a long way since those with a small section for each teacher to comment on a particular pupil. In many cases they form part of a 'profiling' process in which the report contributes towards a wider assessment, or, in more recent developments where 'records of achievement' in school have supplanted traditional reports altogether.

Records of Achievement are a means of compiling a continuous profile of the positive experiences and attainments, reached by each individual child. The resulting document becomes the property of the pupil when he leaves school and is intended as an additional dimension to a pupil's formal school reference. This system allows for pupils to assess themselves and make negotiated statements with their tutors or teachers about their progress. Parental involvement may also be built into the programme. In this way credit may be given for the outside interests, hobbies and personal achievements which might never normally be taken into account by a school.

Nevertheless, it is likely, at least once a year, that you will be asked to compile a written report on each pupil in each group you take. At first, this will seem a daunting task. However, if you are asked to write more than one year set of reports simultaneously (unless you teach more than one group in a particular year) this might be regarded as a sign of mismanagement in a school and it is likely to elicit loud criticisms from colleagues in the staffroom!

Some colleagues prefer to tackle the task by a method known as 'topping and tailing'. This merely involves filling in the details of name, class set and so on at the top of the report form (most are of this format) and signing it at the bottom, leaving the space for the comment to be completed later. Then, when this process is finished the reports can be written minus the tedium of adding the necessary information. Many different approaches are possible – choose one which reduces the pressure on you and enables you to do the best for your pupils.

Your comments should always be positive where possible even when criticism is called for: if there are weaknesses ensure that these are rectifiable by effort on the part of the pupil. *Never* use invective or demonstrate dislike, sarcasm or negative personal feelings on a report. Firstly, it is unprofessional, secondly it is destructive and thirdly you are never really aware of the audience to which it is to be addressed. Not only will the child and his/her parent read it, but other colleagues, possibly the Headteacher or other senior staff, likely employers or any other individual or agency. Once you have written it the report becomes common currency.

As with comments referred to in the section on 'marking' form your report around the following three functions, therefore:

(1) Make a statement indicating a level of satisfaction with progress made during the year.
(2) Highlight areas of technical difficulty, or those which require some effort or work to rectify, offering advice on the best way to achieve this.
(3) Indicate goals which it might be appropriate to meet in the coming year, giving pleasant encouragement towards meeting these.

Note: In a final, leaving report, it is appropriate to wish the pupil good luck in his or her future career or further education, and any other good wishes you may wish to convey.

If a student is clearly underachieving or has misbehaved, or been a nuisance during the year, convey *disappointment not anger*; clearly state that it is not satisfactory, but always indicate ways in which improvement may be effected. *Find something to praise* as well. For example, Michael may have behaved in an immature way in the course of the year, and cause you intense irritation, but he has an engaging sense of humour and makes you smile. Be critical in a constructive sense by all means, but find something to praise, too. The most difficult or objectionable student will always have some aspect of worth – locate it and make use of it. The exercise at the end of this chapter might be found useful in focusing your ideas.

Making referrals

All schools will have a recognised system for referring instances of poor behaviour or lack of effort, often using the pupil's form tutor as a pivotal point for dealing with problems. At this stage, it is worth examining the options open to you regarding, for example, unacceptable behaviour:

(1) Do nothing.
(2) Make it clear you do not like it and create a framework within which improvement may be made.
(3) Discuss with colleagues, or a senior member of staff informally.
(4) Refer formally.

By the time a behaviour is causing concern, it is likely that option 1 has been overtaken by events, so we will put that to one side. 2 has worth and should be put into action at an early stage anyway, as pupils need to have clear guidelines laid down by you as to what constitutes acceptable and unacceptable behaviour.

As for 3, it is always good practice to discuss matters with another colleague – there is always someone on a staff (not necessarily the person assigned to staff development or probationary induction) to whom you can turn to for advice. Do not be afraid to admit that you are having trouble with a pupil and maintain an open mind on matters of advice. Use that advice to attempt to tackle the problem yourself. Never be tempted to wish the problem away by hoping that 'someone else', whoever that may be, will spirit the pupil, and thus the problem, away. It is usually only at a very late stage that a pupil may become totally uncontrollable and at that stage he will manifestly have to be removed; but at all earlier stages consider the strategies discussed elsewhere in this book.

One final point: all teachers, no matter how senior and/or experienced, will have experienced difficulty with a pupil or group at some stage in their careers (perhaps more recently than you may be aware). Having problems with a pupil or a group is *not* a sign of impending failure or incompetence. No one will ever condemn you for this, and if they should do so, they are indulging in hypocrisy of the worst sort. You are far more likely to find yourself in difficulty by allowing such a problem to fester unresolved or by failing to recognise it for what it is. Always find someone with whom to discuss your difficulties.

Conclusions

Many of the administrative tasks you are asked to do during an average school year may appear to be repetitive, unnecessary or futile. Perhaps some might be, but experiencing this feeling towards them is probably the result of the purpose of such tasks not having been explained fully to you. Many of the tensions felt in contemporary schools can perhaps be attributed to a lack of 'ownership' of ideas or procedures by junior staff. You are perfectly entitled to question why, for example, a particular procedure is necessary at a given time of year, especially so if the reason is not readily apparent. A responsive management structure should always react positively to constructive criticism anyway. This is an important point which cannot be overstressed: if you do have reason to criticise or question, couch it in positive terms and suggest alternative approaches. You will soon gain a reputation as a positive thinker, and, incidentally, be taken more seriously.

PRACTICAL TASK EIGHT

You may find it helpful to practice your technique of report writing by completion of the following examples, which illustrate three differing instances of pupil behaviour and performance. Try, if you can, to avoid cliché or a standardised format. This is more easily achieved by visualising each pupil carefully as if seated in front of you when you are compiling the report. Think of his/her strengths and positive achievements first before embarking on constructive criticism.

If at all possible avoid these clichés or extreme value judgements (all of which have been seen recently on written reports).

must try/work harder, satisfactory, unsatisfactory, unacceptable, stupid, boring, irritating, pathetic, moronic.

Example (1)

Julie, a year ten G.C.S.E. pupil, average ability. Julie has missed some of your lessons this year owing to having contracted glandular fever in the Autumn term. She is a popular and lively member of your group although inclined to waste time by gossiping with others. She stands a good chance of achieving a G.C.S.E. grade if she adopts certain strategies for the rest of the course. For this and the other two examples you may find useful the format given as Figure 1.

Figure 1

Name	Tutor Group	Subject
		Teacher

Signed ....

Date ....

Example (2)

Gary is a year nine pupil. He is in an all-ability group which includes one 'statemented' child. He has obvious potential and will achieve excellence with encouragement. Unfortunately the ethos and behaviour of this group (for reasons outside your control) militates against a pupil being seen to work hard. Write Gary's report, giving examples of strategies which might help him.

Example (3)

A slightly different approach: Sammy is in your year seven tutor group. He is from a one parent family. His parent is most anxious for him to do well at his new secondary school. Unfortunately Sammy has had difficulty in settling into the school and doesn't make relationships with peers or staff very easily.

Your school offers pupils a facility for self-assessment and Sammy has already observed these facts himself and actively seeks help.

Write a tutor report on Sammy which is constructive, supportive, yet offers some strategies he can follow in the coming term.

CHAPTER 6

Referrals to Outside Agencies

The basic tenet underpinning this handbook is the belief that unwanted behaviour in the classroom can, in the majority of cases, be prevented by sound classroom management. The previous chapters deal with how to understand and manage the situations you may be confronted with, where you can absorb and effectively deal with the majority of difficult times that occur. However, in every school and almost in every class, there will occasionally be the time when another perspective is needed. This intervention from another person may range from having a 'second opinion' or advice on alternative procedures, through to wanting the outside agency to 'take the problem away'.

What is an outside agency? Who are they? How do they function? When are they not appropriate? What are their limitations? These and the crucially important aspects of information exchange and pre-referral procedures are now developed.

Outside agencies are, as their name suggests, people with specific expertise from outside the usual confines of the school. Their input is restricted to occasions when internal strategies have been tried or when an additional support is needed to supplement the internal methods.

Preliminary stages

Secondary schools have highly structured pastoral systems with which to deal with the many situations which arise from day to day. Classroom based difficulties ascend through the system at a speed dictated by the seriousness of the initial offence, efficiency of intervention along the way and competence of all the staff dealing with the situation. In some cases, problems which arise out of the local classroom routine are completely dealt with by the professional on site, i.e. the teacher in charge of that session. That teacher sees his or her role as stopping most difficulties as they arise and thus not allowing them to grow and get out of hand. Senior members of staff are not required for the majority of incidents thereby allowing them to deal with more urgent and serious matters. The teacher who can command respect and control in his/her classroom environment and use the senior staff only as and when required enjoys the satisfaction of being in total control. However this does not preclude asking for advice and opinions particularly from more experienced members of staff.

Some teachers use the internal pastoral system rather more quickly than is justified and find that the offence within the classroom soon becomes unnecessarily serious with the involvement of senior staff members. The result is often a diminution of respect for the class teacher concerned and a devaluing of the pastoral system of which every teacher is a member. The dividing line between solving your own problems and passing them on within the internal pastoral system needs to be dealt with sensitively. One does not like to be seen to be failing to cope and therefore there is a tendency to cover up the reality of a situation. One needs to remember that all teachers experience a feeling of failure from time to time and therefore the need to conceal the problem is not necessary.

There are going to be occasions when referral along the pastoral line is needed and the first stop is often your Head of Department, who will always want to be informed of matters arising, even if small and seemingly insignificant. This apparently self-contradictory statement can be explained as follows. To inform your Head of Department of relevant information, knowing that you are controlling the situation makes for a supportive, caring team approach to problem solving. When it is therefore necessary to involve further stages of the pastoral support team, those members know from which perspective the referral is coming. By discussing situations with your colleagues as they arise, you establish an ethos of team work.

There will be occasions when more serious incidents require input from senior staff. The use of these members, the support they give, and indeed receive, and the methods they employ for problem solving and crisis intervention are the scope for a later chapter. It is sufficient to say that when the use of an outside agency is contemplated many, if not all, well-proven internal pastoral strategies will have been tried and may well have met with differing amounts of success.

That is not to say that outside agencies are only needed when everything else has failed. They have a very valuable role of supplementing intervention and providing alternative perspectives. For example, an Education Welfare Officer (E.W.O.) might be asked to make a supportive home visit to establish ways in which a school might attempt to improve attendance well before the stage where it has deteriorated. From an internal perspective especially, great importance needs to be given to the support and communication necessary for working such systems. They are a general pre-requisite in order to develop much more efficient working practices. These are enhanced by closer and more regular contact with the school at all levels, from discussion with the Head and Senior Management to direct help with classroom teachers and support staff. Effective communication at all levels with all people is crucial.

Teachers are practical people and need practical solutions with practical help. Some will demand the problem be removed (a very practical solution for the teacher but not necessarily the best for the whole system). Some will want practical help in different ways and it must be recognised that encouragement, support, new strategies for managing situations and using 'coping skills', all constitute practical help. The practical solutions have to be relevant, effective, supportive (of teacher and pupil), and to the mutual benefit of all components within the system.

Some fundamental principles

In looking at the internal devices and possible involvement from outside agencies we need to remind ourselves of some fundamental principles to educating children and young people. In 1978 the Warnock Report on Special Education argued that children with problems whether physical, emotional or intellectual should, as far as possible, remain within the mainstream of education. Children who exhibit special needs of any kind are frequently met with in the classroom and often find their difficulties erupting to the surface in the classroom. While it is hard work to control difficult behaviour in the classroom, it is in the interests of the pupil to do so. In addition to stating the need for such children to be educated within mainstream provision, the Warnock Report detailed the process by which assessment is to be made within the school prior to involvement of outside agencies.

> Stage one involves . . . the class teacher or form tutor will consult the Headteacher . . . will be responsible for marshalling all the infor-

mation... will take a decision to make special arrangements for the pupil within the competence of the school or to continue their education without change but subject to further review, or to seek further advice.

Stage two involves the child's difficulties being discussed with a teacher with training and expertise in special education... 'the Headteacher will... be responsible for... all the available information... or the teacher with special expertise or the advisory teacher may carry out a further assessment of the child's needs... in addition, the prescription of a special programme may be supervised by the specialist or advisory teacher.' (Warnock)

These two important stages begin a referral process and, if performed accurately, form a sound foundation for information exchange with outside agencies. This baseline of knowledge is crucial to effective outside agency support and possible intervention.

What is an outside agency?

There is much that schools can do internally in providing expertise with which to combat youngsters' unwanted difficult classroom behaviour. There will be occasions however, when another perspective or further information is needed to supplement the schools' view. There will also be times when the school are looking for support from any area in order to help them hold onto the youngster. There will still be some schools who will want the outside agency to take the problem away or sanction the removal to another establishment. In all these cases the people who are brought into the school can all be called outside agencies. They will have a different viewpoint from the school's. For example, while some teachers may wonder about having the G.P. in to discuss a pupil's progress, that doctor may well have in his/her possession another piece of the jigsaw with which to complete the whole.

Representatives of outside agencies have a professional responsibility which focuses on the youngster (or their family) in a different way to that of the school. Schools educate young people. They are providers of knowledge, creators and harnessers of intellectual, emotional and physical growth. They cannot be all things to all people and need to use outside contacts for support, advice and sometimes practical help. Before we list these agencies and give an outline of their role, let us look at why they are involved in schools and the reasons for referral.

Why use outside agencies?

Some years ago a piece of research was completed as part of the Kent Family Placement Project (Hazel 1981), looking at foster placements and how youngsters who were fostered, were helped to settle at school. The findings showed quite clearly the importance of good relationships at the administrative level within the school. Also that the school's senior management had to have a vested interest in order to facilitate the effective placement. The Kent Family Placement Project highlighted an effective partnership developed between the school and the outside agencies. School placements were made in consultation with a variety of interested parties who had something positive to offer. Face-to-face collaboration was needed and supported. This in turn helped teachers show imagination and flexibility in helping the young people 'catch up' and prevent truancy.

In 1982, John Bald, Tutor in Charge of Essex Education Department Reading and Language Centre, set up an experiment to look at children's reading. (Bald, 1982). His idea was to improve constructive communication between teachers and social workers by providing a clear and mutually accepted point of focus; in this particular case, the provision of consistent adult support for reading. He used residential social workers to give directed, planned time to listening to a child read in the home setting. The focus was to improve reading skills. The teachers could see that a practical session of hearing children read proved an excellent way for the residential social worker to get to know the youngsters in their care. There were definite advantages for the school, in that vital skills preparation on a one-to-one basis was being carried out regularly with the obvious positive repercussions in the school curriculum.

There is a wealth of expertise available to schools which can be utilized by sensitive and forward thinking management. Communication is critical in this inter-agency work and will be returned to again and again. It is sufficient at this stage to say that it is important to share relevant information between interested parties. It is equally important to share information as an ongoing process and not as a once and for all experience at the time of crisis. It is easy to concentrate efforts on communication at the point of real need but in order to facilitate the 'whole view' approach to young people's needs, information appertaining to them and their position in life needs to circulate to relevant people at other times as well. This, while not wanting to create feelings of intrusion, is an excellent way of keeping up to date and being a caring professional who is in control of their work and responsibility. Clearly such an approach to monitoring young people needs careful and thoughtful consideration. As an aid to the preventative approach to behaviour management it is a very valuable tool.

Who are the outside agencies?

It could be argued that outside agencies fall into three main categories: Education, Social Services and others. Each have their own professional responsibility and consequently a different viewpoint on the difficulty presented. Each will be able to offer alternative thoughts and opinions; some will not be welcome but all must be heard and assimilated to the benefit of the whole. Roles and responsibilities will vary from area to area. The following is intended to provide an outline list of the provision known to the authors. It is an open-ended list with other areas of the country having different types of provision, with perhaps different names and different working practices.

Education

The Education Department offer many specialist workers who cover the range of specific learning difficulties encountered by youngesters in school. From the management services at county level to the face to face contact of the one-to-one teaching situation, there is a wealth of provision. All are equally professional and each is specifically trained to address the specific difficulty being encountered. Most of the area or local services come under the Area Education Office and Chief Officer. They have the ability to mobilise staff from their office and will be represented on inter-agency meetings, governors' meetings and so on. The Area Education Officer, or their Deputy, will give the authority's view and policy on matters relating to schools and will follow the Warnock recommendations that 'wherever possible, young people who exhibit special needs will be educated within the mainstream of schools.' With this as their baseline, they will have access to the specialist personnel needed to carry out such a function.

One such early intervention team is the Education Welfare Service who will have an officer assigned to a number of schools; this is the officer who used to be called 'the school policeman' and had an image of running after youngsters and pushing them back into school. Happily this perception has changed and they are at the forefront of the intervention when home related difficulties occur or non-attendance is becoming a concern.

The Educational Psychologist is an accessing agent to specialist help, particularly for those young people who have attainment difficulties. They are the coordinators of the Multi-Professional Assessment referral system for statementing children and young people and they recommend the appropriate course of action based upon the reports written by the various agencies contained within the assessment. Advisory teams and Support Teachers are often based in Area Education offices and teachers' centres respectively and, as their title suggests, they work together to focus on the child related problem, devise a package of support and then put it into practice with the class teacher.

Special Schools' Outreach is a facility where teachers employed on special school sites are released from the timetable at certain set times to work within the local mainstream school. This may be to support the passage of a youngster back to that school, or it may involve support of the class teacher where new skills can be acquired and different teaching methods explored.

The Home Tuition Service caters for those who, for a period of time, cannot be educated within the mainstream. There are a variety of reasons why the home tutor provision is an important part of agency work. It has traditionally been the source of statutory provision of ten hours education per week for young people who have long term illness, who have become pregnant, who are school phobics, etc. This has been widened to cater for long term non-school attendance and permanent exclusion cases. The Home Tutor Service is a valuable provision but needs to be a means to an end and not the often inevitable end in itself.

The Youth Service, while under Education, has at its disposal, the vast resources of the Community Education sector. Increasingly, in the authors' county, Community Education is bridging the gap between schools and the community. The community resources with their variety of expertise and opportunity, can be used by a school and thereby provide another educational function and perspective.

At present the arrangements outlined above are typical of many L.E.A.s. Recent legislation resulting in Local Management of Schools (L.M.S.) may cause these arrangements to change. One consequence might be that some schools may wish to make greater use of these services by purchasing them, whilst others may choose to spend their delegated budget on alternative provision.

Social Services

Social Services generally offer a family-based viewpoint and focus their attention on the way the young person relates to the family and surrounding conditions. The Area Social Services Office is run by an Area Officer who controls and guides a range of specialist provision to be called upon whenever conditions dictate. The main agents for statutory work and referral are the Generic Social Workers, whose case load may contain clients from all age groups. As they operate on the first tier of provision, they are often extremely over-worked but they are backed up by the support teams. These focus on specific issues and difficulties.

Their social work perspective is clearly upon the youngster and will put their attentions on home based difficulties before anything else. Youngsters often take these difficulties into school with them and therefore it is essential that social workers and teachers are concerned with coordinating very closely on paths that converge towards the ultimate aim, that of having a happy, balanced, individual, receiving their usual educational experience.

In all work with outside agencies, the overall aim is to develop a corporate plan. This will only happen if all parties concerned see the overall focus and do not let professional differences and alternative perspectives cloud progress. Residential Social Workers are 'parents' in the Family Centre setting. They have a statutory responsibility for the young people in their care and they can be effectively used. Sonia Jackson (1987) while referring to foster parent placements commented that the foster parents' relatively high level of education and confidence proved very useful in enabling them to negotiate with the schools and sometimes to intercede for the young people in their charge... 'This must, in our opinion, equally refer to paid employees of a local authority who can impart their unique role as professional parents and thereby have an excellent creative input to schools.'

Young Offenders Teams are resource teams who monitor, evaluate and support young people who show offending behaviour and come into the usual Police jurisdiction. Juvenile Justice Teams operate in a similar way and are very useful colleagues for advice and local support. Their knowledge of Juvenile Justice local regimes and County and National trends can be helpful in providing another perspective. Intermediate Treatment Teams are geared specifically to work with offenders and provide face to face work with individuals often in group settings. Again their viewpoint can be most helpful and supportive, if only it is sought.

Another very important team with the social services is the Child Resource Team. These, among their many possible functions, coordinate foster parent placements and give insight into 'hidden' areas of need, that sometimes need bringing to the attention of schools.

In all these cases, the specialist teams are available for advice and possible support. There are reserves of resource which are often untapped. Advice is non-committing, is only a telephone call away and is specialised.

Other outside agencies

As outlined already the two main areas for outside agencies are Education and Social Services but there is a range of other important groups who will have a part to play in inter-agency cooperation.

The Police are valuable contributors not solely from looking at offending behaviour, but from an overall community perspective. They can use their statutory knowledge and focus it on community welfare issues.

The Probation Service, while not dealing with the usual school age range, do have input at the age of seventeen and therefore will have something to share with those in the later years at school who give cause for concern.

The Careers Service are excellent providers to schools for guidance in careers potential and possibilities. They are the accessing agents for work experience and have at their disposal a vast resource of employment and work experience opportunities. This is very useful when looking at strategies for maintaining a school placement for a year eleven pupil.

A large area of support comes from the Area Health Authority. Usually the most important representative of this is the Family Practitioner who again is an accessing agent for a variety of specialists. Health matters are of particular importance to a young person at school.

Child Psychiatry and Child Guidance have a role to play also in this very specialised field of working with unwanted behaviour. Social Workers or the G.P. access these facilities and their specific knowledge and expertise can be an asset to the overall view.

Depending upon the area of the country in which you are teaching or anticipating to teach, there will be a plethora of child-centred support groups whose role will be to concentrate on the specific difficulties encountered by individuals in their care. They often offer outreach work because they too will be convinced that the foundation for inter-agency cooperation is that young people with special needs must have those particular needs met in a normal education. Outreach work in this way gets away from the special unit approach and focuses support on the mainstream school. This enhances and supports the intervention approach.

The outside agency concept, in helping the school perform its statutory responsibility, is an open-ended one. There will be other agencies in your area, perhaps not covered here, who can be used to support your school. The secret is to join forces in one unified, corporate approach to solving unwanted behaviour.

How do outside agencies work?

We have mentioned before that the overriding function of inter-agency cooperation is to provide a whole view perspective. This deserves repetition. Individual professionals can often take a narrow view of their client. In calling upon other people, a holistic attitude toward pupil/staff support must predominate. In giving breadth to a service of this type the following aims need to be borne in mind:

- To assist existing support services and agencies in the identification, management and support of young people experiencing difficulties at school.
- To assist schools to develop attitudes, skills, curricula and systems to prevent alienation and disaffection from occurring.
- To establish, through small group and personal tutorial work, healthy, supportive relationships between adults and young people and to prevent or repair attitudes of disaffection and alienation from schools and authority in general.
- To work directly with young people in their schools (as appropriate) in collaboration with school staff as part of a school-based response to problems. This may show itself in an outside agency representative being able to offer something to the school, thereby benefitting both youngster and system. For example in the area of personal counselling and guidance; perhaps assisting them in relationship problems with peers, parents and the community and also with practical problems, for example, homelessness, court appearances, employment and so on.

● To help maintain young people within the mainstream of school and community life.

Bearing in mind these broad aims for inter-agency cooperation, an American study in 1974 led to the development of guidelines to help enlist the cooperation of social work, school, teachers and foster parents. In this study, Canning (1974) identified serious problems of adjustment to school among foster children. This adjustment was often aggravated by different perceptions of purpose by teacher, social worker or parent. Only when they came together with a common purpose, that of ensuring stability and enriching educational experiences for young people, did progress begin.

The foster children's own perspective was very similar to that of a study by the National Association for People in Care (1983). The youngsters were anxious not to be treated as different. They disliked teachers probing into their backgrounds or exposing their situation to peers. They found many aspects of their school life uncomfortable, confusing and distressing. To overcome these difficulties a set of procedures were set up which involved close liaison with all workers concerned with the youngsters, to establish accurate information exchange points, to create and maintain records of achievement and generally to become centred and to break down inter-agency barriers.

Outside agency cooperation then has, at its foundation, the firm belief that a united, corporate approach to problem solving is the only way forward. It is clearly crucial that when different people with alternative perspectives meet to work together, then accurate communication is essential to any further development. The areas of information exchange and communication are dealt with later in the chapter but are worth mentioning here too to ensure that a clear message is received.

The ABC theory of behavioural analysis

Outside agencies may support each other and indeed the schools by looking at the ABC of behavioural analysis. Much work has been done on the Antecedents, Behaviour and Consequences sequence of events and this area is covered more fully in Chapter Seven.

At this point we can observe this 'chain reaction' of behaviour quite simply and briefly by looking at an incident in which unwanted behaviour is the inevitable outcome.

From your experiences so far in the classroom, select an item of unwanted behaviour and fit it to the categories listed below. If you find the first two sections difficult to describe, be aware of the ABC of unwanted behaviour when you are next confronted by a difficulty in your classroom.

Antecedents	*Behaviour*	*Consequences*
Describe precisely	Describe accurately	Describe what
what happened	the child's responses	happened next, e.g.
immediately before		What did you do?
the incident		What did other
		children do?

From this formalised observation stance some plan for removing or altering the antecedent/s may be implemented. Other agencies may be well positioned to contribute to this observation plan. They may hold key clues as to why certain behaviours exhibit themselves in the classroom. A collective discussion of the facts, with an overall viewpoint will enable a corporate plan of action to be developed. In this area of work, many strategies are possible. None will work unless the prime cause is removed. An understanding of ABC behavioural analysis even in its simplest form, is critical to the successful implementation of systems intervention.

When are outside agencies not appropriate?

Schools have at their disposal a variety of internal strategies which may be employed to support the teacher who is having difficulties in the classroom and these are often exhausted before outside help is sought. There are, however, occasions when outside agency support is not appropriate. For example, when the school can effectively use its own resources and provide the satisfactory working answer. Such a position relies heavily upon well motivated and skilled staff who have a real desire to seek workable solutions.

In the Preventative Approach to Disruption (P.A.D.) four basic assumptions were formulated as being a useful, workable baseline for dealing with unwanted behaviours.

(1) The behaviour of teachers influences the behaviour of pupils.
(2) Effective teachers are skilled at avoiding trouble.
(3) Techniques of classroom management can be identified and learned.
(4) Teachers should take responsibility for developing their own skills.

With this approach to teacher awareness and effectiveness, coupled with the Warnock two stages of 'pre outside agency involvement', then schools have a useful resource in their own staff in supporting and managing difficult behaviour in the classroom. Such staff can adapt to the ever changing needs of challenging young people. In-service training and/or a basic common sense to managing difficult behaviour will take the committed teacher into four main areas of controlling difficult situations:

(1) Rules and routines – considering the source and content of school rules, how they are established and maintained.

(2) Avoiding problems – considering the importance of establishing authority, maintaining vigilance and addressing pupils effectively.

(3) De-escalating conflicts – considering the aim of dealing with conflict and a range of interventions and the subsequent relationship between the teacher and the pupil.

(4) Rewards and punishments – considering effective ways of using both in a controlled manner.

It is worth enquiring when it is appropriate to bring in outside agencies. Schools will vary considerably as to their sensitivity on this issue. These other people also may vary considerably as to when they think their intervention is most appropriate. Three intervention criteria can be used to help be objective in assessing when outside input is needed:

● Does the behaviour presumed to be difficult, occur at sufficient strengths? In this context strength is an indication of frequency and duration of the unwanted behaviour.

● Will the behaviour, if continued, harm the pupil and/or his immediate environment? This is an important consideration especially in relation to the safety of staff and pupils.

● Would the behaviour be likely to impede subsequent adaptation and healthy development?

An objective assessment is very important and may be obtained by physically monitoring how often the behaviour occurs, how severe it is and what length of time it lasts. The table at the end of the chapter gives an extract from a behaviour checklist. It goes some way to ensuring a standard approach to discussing difficult behaviour.

This area of work is extremely important because no-one wants difficult behaviour in class and, for a variety of reasons, teachers will respond to it in different ways. This makes an objective assessment very hard to ascertain unless usual monitoring procedures are employed. Teachers can easily become too subjective over what are quite emotional issues found in the class. What may sound a vicious attack, may be in fact horse play or not vicious at all to another. A good example of this was observed in a class as follows:

A youngster was referred because of his 'disruptive' and 'dangerous' behaviour. This youngster had been told to sit out the P.E. lesson because he had no P.E. kit. At the end of the lesson (taken outside on the hard play area) the teacher came over and said, 'There, did you see that? All through the lesson, throwing stones at others.' This was startling to hear since observation of him throughout the lesson did not support it. He had been sitting quietly and in the last five minutes became bored by his exclusion, picked up some gravel from the floor and was playing that old fashioned game of 'snobs'. This involves picking up an object while throwing those in your hand into the air, and subsequently catching them all again. Objective observation, and the busy teacher's perception of what is happening can lead to completely different conclusions.

Using an outside agency is not always appropriate. The general answer to intervention is that people must be aware of the real needs of the situation both from the pupil, staff and school point of view. But at the end of all deliberations, it is upon the young people we must concentrate. It is their needs which have to be met in such a way as to sustain their educational experience in as normal a way as possible.

What are the limitations of outside agencies?

Outside agencies do not have magic answers and are not capable of turning around unwanted behaviour overnight. Some schools, being practical establishments, want practical answers straight away. Comments such as, 'There must be a special school for them, to cater for their needs' or 'What he needs now is a short sharp shock to bring him to his senses,' are made with the best of intentions but are really way off the target. It is at times like those when inter-agency staff need extra resolve to help re-align perspectives and put the whole business onto a firm, objective foundation.

Outside agencies and their limitations can be viewed from studying the diagram at the end of the chapter, where a school's pupil breakdown is matched with various categories of behaviour and the subsequent possible agency action. The table shows that the vast majority of internally containable youngsters come within the area marked by a dotted line. The further up the pyramid the youngster's behaviour value goes, the more outside agencies with specific roles and responsibilities are involved. It could be argued that some outside agency input needs to be limited to protect the young person from becoming too serious a case and thereby creating more serious provision that what was initially required. In this circumstance, it would be easy to view a youngster with certain needs and put him/her in the most appropriate box on the chart. This simplistic approach to managing classroom behaviour must be avoided and is not the tone of the inter agency approach.

Nevertheless, it must be stated that some young people will inevitably find themselves in provision which is outside the expertise of mainstream schools and their usual support agencies. These young people will have at their disposal a number of special units. They will go by many different names apart from the vernacular 'sin bin'; tutorial units, withdrawal units, support units, education guidance centres, day units, off-site support centres, retreat centres, havens and opportunity groups. The fact that there are places for 'problem youngsters' to go to must encourage us to try all other forms of intervention before resorting to the final solution. Sadly, these ultimate placements, even though they perform an excellent service, have a tendency to contain inappropriately placed young people.

General inter agency liaison meetings

In a Midlands education authority, inter-agency liaison groups have been set up to meet every half term as an open forum for debate and discussion. They are not just talking shops but keep to a strict agenda which consists of two main parts. Part one is an opportunity to bring to agencies' notice those young people who the school feel are in need of extra attention. This turns into an information exchange session, where relevant information is shared and discussed and decisions are made for the future. This vital part of the meeting serves to ensure a mutually agreed course of action with agreed roles and responsibilities. This action is beneficial for two reasons. Firstly, awareness has been raised through information exchange and secondly, action is being taken. These meetings would not succeed if the agreed action to be taken was never arrived at.

Action is crucial and outside agencies need to attend meetings knowing that they may have to contribute in some practical way. This may range from a 'one off' piece of advice to a time input commitment.

Part two involves a commitment from the school staff towards their support and training. Inset days are a valuable opportunity for school staff and others to get together and work towards each other with the one common goal. Exercises are devised and questionnaires created and completed-periods of relaxed in-depth study of each other's role all serve to bind together a variety of professionals, experts in their field. For better understanding and cooperation, groups need to consider the following types of questions:

● What do we assume and what do we actually know about each other's jobs and attitudes?
● What do we expect of each other currently?
● Where are expectations not met?
● Given an understanding of the availability of resources on both sides, what could be improved?

This joint commitment to gain more understanding and come closer together with a corporate mechanism for managing difficult behaviour is crucial and is illustrated by a piece of research by David Galloway, an Educational Psychologist (Trends 1979). 'The likelihood of a secondary school pupil being excluded or referred for special school depends at least as much, and probably more, on the particular school he/she happens to attend, as on any constitutional factors affecting his/her behaviour.' Bearing this in mind, this large area of uncharted territory where schools and outside agencies come together for mutual support and to devise an effective and corporate plan, needs to be mapped, adventured into and conquered.

Referrals and reports

We have seen how important it is to get together and develop our collective plan of action. This final outcome to what may be many expensive hours of professional work is in jeopardy if, in the beginning, and running all the way through the process, accuracy, objectivity, authenticity and confidentiality are not key issues to information exchange whether it is for referring cases and raising others' awareness or in writing reports for statutory bodies.

● All statements must be established as objective fact.
● Be aware of using adjectives/adverbs – the value they imply and the elements of personal judgement they involve.

- Be continually on your guard against imparting your opinions on others. Stick with the facts.
- Be aware of who may see this written word and how long it will remain on file.
- Consider the danger and implications of what you say or write.
- Keep the report focussed on the issues with accurate and relevant information.
- Can you justify the comments given?

The authors conducted a small piece of research among twenty-two secondary schools in their areas of work within Derbyshire. These schools were approached and circulated with a questionnaire, the aim of which was to gain information about existing communication systems and to establish whether those in daily contact with other agencies perceived a need for a single standardised format. Predictably, most returns stated that informal telephone contacts were widely used, whilst there seemed some confusion over the range of paperwork currently available. Others were concerned about any move towards increased bureaucracy, perhaps misunderstanding our motives. However, the vast majority agreed that a standardised form of communication would be helpful.

The final result of this action is that:

(1) The originating institution has a record of not only its own actions on a pupil/client, but the response/actions of all other relevant agencies.
(2) The receiving agencies have a clear picture of the actions of the originating institutions and have acknowledged their own actions and response.
(3) Even if group action such as a case conference is not con-templated, there has been an exchange of information.
(4) If, by any chance, the receiving agency can make no subsequent use of the information, it can be destroyed, if appropriate.

We felt that the survey established a need for such inter-agency communication and that its use would be most effective, help alleviate confusion, enhance inter-agency relationships and make objective communication more formal. We made it extremely clear that such use of a form was not intended to destroy informal contacts but that the goodwill generated by the sharing of information would enhance them.

Writing reports, showing information to be accurate, objective and focussed all arise out of a desire to work diligently towards the goal of providing a caring, nurturing, developing educational experience for those with whom we are charged. It is our responsibility to overcome the occasional professional barriers between each other in order to provide the effective, corporate plan for those young people who have difficulties in the classroom and beyond. Carl Rogers (1983) sets the tone for our work together:

> I was eager for teachers to know something of what we have learned so that they would try it for themselves . . . We had found a way of being with students that was sharply different from conventional education. It did not involve teaching so much as it involved us in a process that we came to think of as the facilitation of learning. It involved a deep trust in students, rather than the distrust prevalent in many classrooms. It involved an attempt to be with the learner in a number of ways. It meant being with the student in a sensitive understanding of his or her own interests, desires and directions. It involved being a real person in the student teacher relationship, rather than playing a role.

BEHAVIOUR CHECKLIST

Please estimate your view of the student/pupil for each dimension by marking one box most appropriate to the behaviour observed.

Positive Dimensions				Negative Dimensions		
Always	Frequently	Sometimes	Mid point	Sometimes	Frequently	Always
+3	+2	+1	0	−1	−2	−3

The negative ratings equate to the opposite dimension

General Attitude	+3	+2	+1	0	−1	−2	−3

Attends school
Attends my lessons
Happy re school
On time to school
On time to class
No complaints physically
Appears confident
Conforms to school rules
Responds well to corrrection
Parents support school
Student cares about parents'
view of performance

Classroom Behaviour

On task re class work
Remains in place
Controls self well
Finds next task well
Settles down quickly
Relaxed when working
Good concentration
Speaks/answers appropriately
Respects others' property
Respects peers

Attitude to Teacher/Work

Follows Teacher's instructions
Enjoys new situations
Makes positive remarks to Teacher
Works well independently
Shows interest in work
Completes set tasks
Co-operative to Teacher

Attitude to Peers

Is fair to peers
Interested in others
Sociable/co-operates well
Does not bully others
Communicates well with peers
Not aggressive to peers

PUPIL BEHAVIOUR AND INTERVENTION SYSTEMS

This diagram is NOT drawn to scale and only shows the pyramid of provision available. Each section does NOT indicate quantity of need of difficulty.

Key to initials:

MC   –   Major Crime
MI   –   Mental Illness
YC   –   Youth Custody
APU   –   Adolescent Psychiatric Unit
MPA   –   Multi Professional Assessment (Statementing)
NSA   –   Non School Atttendance
Res Ed   –   Residential Education

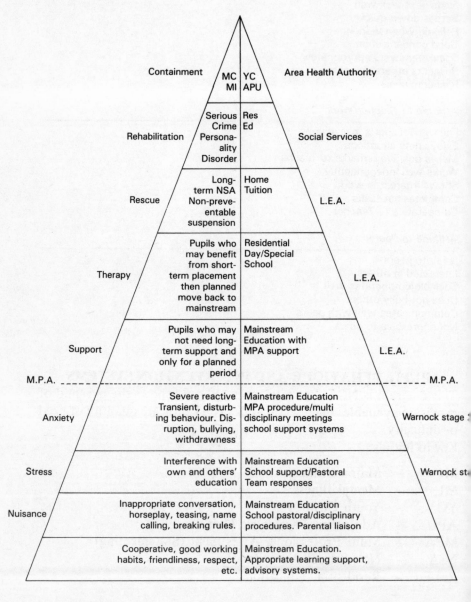

Behaviour Value   Action/Provision

Behaviour Value			Action/Provision
Containment	MC MI	YC APU	Area Health Authority
Rehabilitation	Serious Crime Personality Disorder	Res Ed	Social Services
Rescue	Long-term NSA Non-preventable suspension	Home Tuition	L.E.A.
Therapy	Pupils who may benefit from short-term placement then planned move back to mainstream	Residential Day/Special School	L.E.A.
Support	Pupils who may not need long-term support and only for a planned period	Mainstream Education with MPA support	L.E.A.
M.P.A.			M.P.A.
Anxiety	Severe reactive Transient, disturbing behaviour. Disruption, bullying, withdrawness	Mainstream Education MPA procedure/multi disciplinary meetings school support systems	Warnock stage
Stress	Interference with own and others' education	Mainstream Education School support/Pastoral Team responses	Warnock st
Nuisance	Inappropriate conversation, horseplay, teasing, name calling, breaking rules.	Mainstream Education School pastoral/disciplinary procedures. Parental liaison	
	Cooperative, good working habits, friendliness, respect, etc.	Mainstream Education. Appropriate learning support, advisory systems.	

CHAPTER 7

Dealing with Unwanted Behaviour

The term 'unwanted behaviour' is full of evocative feelings and subjective opinions. What may be unwanted to one teacher may be quite acceptable to another. In your first few terms of teaching you will experience from your colleagues different attitudes and tolerances to this area of classroom control. Some will see their role as a teacher of their subject as the primary reason for having pupils in class. Others will place that in a wider educational context and be part of the process of teaching for life. In all cases, effective control over the teaching groups is essential and is brought about by a variety of methods.

In attempting to deal with unwanted behaviour in class you need to be clear about its identification. This chapter will look more closely at behavioural analysis where insight is given to the 'A B C' approach and what 'behaviourism' as a concept has to offer. This is then followed by a review of practical approaches to behaviour management as a preventative technique. Clearly there are times when all the prevention possible does not alleviate the crisis time when a situation explodes. However, some approaches will be detailed for dealing with crisis intervention. Obviously, changing behaviour is a long-term process and therefore we conclude the chapter by looking at how to work with long-term difficulties. These three areas: prevention, crisis intervention and long-term issues all form a continuum of need. The point at which you, as a new teacher fit into that continuum, only you can decide. The guide which follows is designed to help you make your decision.

What is unwanted behaviour?

Behaviour unwanted by one teacher may be completely normal and non-threatening to another. Immediately, therefore, we are confronted by a subjective term which regularly throws teachers off balance. In attempting to identify unwanted behaviour let us use another term; that of disruption. Disruption is more easily defined in that when it occurs in class it interrupts usual, normal class routines. A child continually talking, a pupil staring out of the window and waving to others, a chair 'flying' across the room. All these incidents are potentially disruptive and all have different 'disruption values' depending upon which teacher is in charge. All those incidents are the result of unwanted behaviour and whilst some may be considered normal and harmless, others could be potentially dangerous.

Whatever the causes of the resulting behaviour, these pupils usually provoke aversive reactions or feelings of inadequacy in teachers. Such pupils may exhibit one or more of the following:

- be unable to conform to teacher expectations
- be unable to cope with the group dynamics
- be unhappy or frightened or insecure
- be unable to make sound relationships
- be intolerant
- be poorly motivated
- be suffering from poor self image/self esteem
- be self-centred
- be failing academically

The list is open ended in that there are many reasons for exhibiting unwanted behaviour in class. What you see as the teacher in charge is the manifestation of that behaviour: clearly to ensure progress for individuals in the group, you must tackle this at source.

Identification

In identifying the problem be careful to do just that, i.e. identify the problem behaviour and not the problem child. It is tempting when confronted with something we do not want, to label pupils as being 'problem kids'. This is wrong because they are children who are experiencing difficulties. You may attribute traits to an individual, but be careful here, too, because there is a danger of attaching a convenient label to the child so that we can categorize the problem more easily. For example, that pupil is maladjusted, disturbed, hyperactive, psychotic, neurotic and so on.

Unfortunately if we use these categories we are left with the following problems:

- All the terms suggest different things to different people.
- None of them describe the behaviour or its intensity.
- All the terms leave the problem with the child and distance us from him.
- All firmly label the child.

The argument here is not whether the terms should be used or not but about taking care not to fall into the 'subjectivity trap'. We all use terms for ease of explanation. It is essential for you not to label pupils and see them as 'disruptive', but as young people with difficulties. Far fewer problems are encountered if you study and categorize the behaviour and then look at the surrounding issues which may be affecting it. You are then looking at the disruption itself and not leaving the total responsibility with the pupil. This is borne out by a definition of disruption (Coulby and Harper, 1985) which states that 'Disruption is the product of a school context in which the child is only one of the participants.' That firmly takes some of the responsibility away from the youngster and places it upon you and your colleagues. Rutter *et al.* (1979) state that 'Schools can, and do, have considerable positive effect on the performance and behaviour of their pupils.' We must never lose sight of our importance in this regard.

As teachers we react to pupils' behaviour as it affects us. We need to look at the pupil and the way in which that pupil affects the dynamics of the group, simultaneously avoiding the temptation to be drawn into the hasty, immediate conclusions which may be wrong. Difficulties exhibited often appear as a complex tangle of information and anecdotes. If difficulties are to be identified effectively then they must be seen clearly. This means separating them from the peripheral, irrelevant, often subjective issues. The first step is to define the problem objectively, that is, as being 'that which is confined to empirical evidence.' If you strip away the emotional, subjective issues, you will see the difficulty accurately. By looking objectively you will concentrate on its character within the youngster's present environment. This can be further broken down into antecedents (that which happened before) and consequences (what happened as a result of the behaviour under scrutiny). These terms will be discussed more fully later.

Objectivity, however, is not the sole criterion. The problem identified must also be one that is rectifiable. This is where you as a teacher are central in effecting change. In an earlier chapter we have said that teachers are practical people who want practical advice to practical situations. You are often the best placed person to affect the remedial process. This is why schools are seen to be great 'effectors of change'.

Another benefit is that problems come in batches. It is unusual for a pupil or group who present difficulties to present them one at a time. When problems come in batches you will have to establish a priority or a set of priorities and pick the issue that causes the most trouble before targeting that which you feel most capable of tackling. This ensures some movement toward the goal of eliminating the unwanted behaviour.

To help with identifying unwanted behaviour, list some characteristics of pupils who exhibit behaviours such as: aggressive, passive, assertive. What are the differences between the three categories, especially between aggressive and assertive behaviours? How would you *begin* to deal with each one?

Behaviour is a relative term; behaviour exhibited outside the classroom is often not appropriate once the class has assembled and a lesson begun. Other factors affecting behaviour which need to be borne in mind when making an objective identification are those of:

(1) Peer pressure – when other members of the class, team or group control an individual's response.

(2) Bravado and bullying – when fear will make a pupil behave differently.

(3) Self image – when to 'keep up' with peers is more important than conforming to usual classroom discipline.

(4) Boundary checking – when a pupil will test a situation, or you, to see how you respond. This will always happen with any new teacher. You will be no exception and you will need to be aware of how this will affect the pupils' usual behaviour.

(5) Relationships – between each other as pupils, and the pupil/teacher relationship will affect behaviour and subsequent control.

These are just a few of the factors which may affect the behaviour you are trying to identify. In order to be objective in your observations, note three components to any unwanted behaviour:

● Duration – how long is the behaviour lasting – one minute, continual?
● Frequency – how often does the behaviour exhibit and when?
● Intensity – how 'strong' is the effect of the behaviour?

These three components begin to help you be objective. Therefore, we would advise you to peel away superficial statements such as, 'He has an alcoholic father,' or, 'Her Mum plays bingo every evening,' and look at the behaviour exhibited. You are now beginning to assess the situation. How you deal with it will be explored following an examination of the A B C of behavioural analysis.

The ABC approach to behaviour management

The letters A B C refer to Antecedents, Behaviour and Consequences and a study of them when looking at unwanted behaviour is a key feature to a behaviourist approach. They concentrate on the pupil's present environment and three questions may be asked:

(1) What is the pupil actually doing? This is being clear about behaviour.
(2) What do we want him or her to do instead? This is a positive and objective intention.
(3) What other factors need to be considered? That is, what is motivating and reinforcing the behaviour?

This systematic approach uses the notion that behaviour arises as a result of antecedents; then that behaviour produces certain consequences. Very often in the classroom you will be involved solely in the behaviour and consequences aspect. It is likely that you will have little control over the antecedents. This is not always the case as we have stated in an earlier chapter; teachers can and do have an influence over a pupil's behaviour in its early stages of development in class. Indeed we sometimes create more difficult behaviour.

In our behaviourist view then, the following model summarises the situation:

$$\text{Antecedent} + \text{Background} + \text{Context} = \text{Behaviour} + \text{Consequences}$$
$$\text{(causes)} \qquad\qquad\qquad \text{(effects)}$$

This model introduces factors over which you will not always be in control. For example the background component in the equation is one where previous learning, or lack of it, may have great effect upon the behaviour such as when the teacher previously taking this group may have been highly ineffective. It is clear that we are products of what has happened to us in the past. We learn to behave through rewards and punishments. These are applied through all aspects of human life, but they differ from society to society. Behaviours which make up society's norms become internalised as standards. The individual becomes the source of their own rewards and punishments (for example, congratulating on politeness and feeling guilty when not). Children have to learn which behaviours are acceptable and which are not. They are not born with these values, they are learned from very early days. From a learning theory viewpoint there are two main reasons why some children present behaviour problems:

● Children vary in how quickly they profit from learning.
● Children vary in the quality and quantity of learning experiences they have been exposed to. (That is, home and parents).

These can result in faulty learning and begin to explain the importance of background within the equation.

In explaining some of the bases of faulty learning linked to unwanted behaviour, it is clear that as a teacher within a school setting, you are in a strong position to help remediate the behaviour. Four reasons explain the important position you and the school play in controlling the unwanted behaviour:

(1) Learning does not end with childhood. It continues through life and therefore pupils can, and do, 'unlearn' unwanted behaviour. Opportunities for appropriate learning are created in schools.
(2) The learning approach is about being prospective, working positively towards the future.
(3) Difficult behaviours are not eliminated overnight. Steady, step by step progress is needed towards a stable level of acceptable behaviour.
(4) Teachers and schools are effective agents for socialisation and instruments for change because they provide systematic learning experiences. This implies remedial work as an engine to effect change.

The 'antecedents and context' components of the equation are often observable factors either first hand or by questioning other pupils about an incident and cross checking for accuracy. This part of your work in understanding the behaviour and creating the correct remediable atmosphere depends upon clear, concise, objective accounting of the facts. Make sure if you seek information from others to cross reference it for accuracy. Young people are quite capable of disseminating misinformation and being manipulative. Be careful not to get entangled with rumour, half truth and subjective appraisals made by others.

It is almost always possible to find by objective observation, recording and analysis both antecedents and consequences to specified behaviour problems. Take the following account of an incident and prepare the Antecedents, Behaviour (problematic) and Consequences for it:

> Albert is a thirteen year old boy with moderate learning difficulties who receives five hours of 'statemented' help each week from a support teacher, specially appointed to the school staff for his benefit. His domestic background is very poor, with a stepfather who suffers from mental illness and a mother who spends time in the company of other men. Albert produced bizarre and aggressive behaviour, particularly when running down the corridor on the way in from the hard play area with other noisy, poorly socialised pupils. On this occasion he was uncontainable and showed problems just like those of an older brother who used to attend the school. Albert entered the classroom, refused to sit down when told and ran about until his teacher caught up with him and forced him to sit down. He seemed to gain pleasure from the response of those around him. Efforts to enlist the support of his parents met with statements of good intention but most inadequate action.

Now prepare your A B C analysis of the above situation.

The compiler of this report has allowed himself to compromise any possibility of viewing the *actual* problem by the use of subjective material. The *objective* analysis would read as follows:

Antecedents:
- On the way in from the hard play area ...
- with his noisy friends
- all running down the corridor
- Albert enters the classroom

Behaviour:
- and (regularly and predictably) runs around the room
- laughing and shouting
- knocking over furniture and
- refuses to sit down when told to

Consequences:
- His teacher chases after him
- and forces him to sit in his seat
- The other pupils are laughing.

This kind of analysis, when applied to prioritized problem behaviour provides the opportunity for staff to plan coherent interventions. You will notice that nothing has been retained about Albert's family, the comparison to his older brother or the difficulty in gaining parental support. None of these is relevant to this analysis and it is unclear as to the value they have in planning positive action. Therefore, avoid such subjective statements in your assessment of the difficulty.

Further practice in selecting objective statements with the A B C analysis approach can be had by choosing from your own experiences in class, a situation where such information is available and categorising it in terms of Antecedents, Behaviour and Consequences. With practice you will learn to be objective in identification and assessment.

When analysed in this way, behaviour can be controlled by using, for example, a behaviour modification approach. This applies positive reinforcement in the form of ticks, stars, merits, credits and other rewards. These are awarded for behaviour which conforms to that which the teacher has agreed with the pupil. The accumulation of these 'incentives' can be used in conjunction with a reward system agreed with the parents. For example, a trip out, or a special treat. All tasks can be rewarded by praise but avoid highlighting the absence of credits/ticks for some children. Breaking classroom/teacher rules could result in, initially, a firm reminder of the broken rule and subsequently by cancellation of a tick, merit or other reward.

After a period of time the individual programme is run down in response to an improvement in behaviour. This is a useful way of controlling behaviour especially as the parents can be involved in a positive way. Parents are often considered 'uninterested' or 'useless' or unsupportive of the school. This is hardly surprising when they may have had negative experiences of schools themselves. Such experiences are then reinforced by having pastoral heads or other staff reading a list of misdemeanors that their child has committed, with the question, 'And what are you going to do about it?' It is not surprising that parents may feel inadequate in such circumstances. In the case for rewarding behaviour, parents are crucial as part of the team in overcoming problems of behaviour.

The analysis of such behaviour is known as 'behaviourism'. This offers the following:

● It tries to account for all behaviour.
● It is non-labelling.
● It provides the technology for systematic recording of an observable event.

- It provides an analysis to interpret events in terms of antecedent and consequences.
- It provides an invitation for intervention.
- It enables evaluation to be carried out.

In dealing with problem behaviour by such a 'behaviourist' approach the teacher needs to look for strong reinforcers to motivate the pupil into alternative, appropriate courses of action. Of course, this is one approach and may well be met with little success. There is a need to remember the powerful influences exerted upon the child in your class from outside school, from peers and from others' perception of that behaviour. Even after much deliberation and work, the behaviour may still exist, perhaps only being contained rather than eliminated. However, if the problem is approached in a positive, systematic and objective way and you have increased confidence, then tension is likely to be reduced and the behaviour may assume smaller proportions and be easier to handle.

Behaviourist theory is a good technique for dealing with potential long term unwanted behaviour; there is the consideration of having to deal with incidents on a day-to-day basis which occur spontaneously. It would now be prudent to examine this in addition to 'crisis intervention' before moving on to long term issues.

Practical approaches to classroom behaviour management

Teaching, in common with other occupations, depends upon routine and following familiar patterns day by day. The timetable dictates which classes you will see and it is into that pattern you need to fit. We have previously held that teaching is a rewarding career with many benefits; this might not be the case for the teacher who is ill-prepared or who conditions himself to expect trouble with his classes.

One of the hallmarks of an effective teacher in control is preparation. Many crisis situations can be avoided by adequate forethought. Crises will always occur in the best regulated classroom, but your ability to cope with them will be greater if you feel both confident and competent.

Preparation of work has been covered in an earlier chapter. What is vital is to develop concurrently with this the concept of self-preparation. The model reproduced below may help in determining such an approach. It may be found useful to apply it to your own situation.

Organisation: that basic preparation needed before detailed planning
                - time taken to get organised
                - choice and effectiveness of planned strategies
                - setting standards and targets to go for

Planning: the detail of the lesson
                - identification of task
                - identification and use of skills
                - use of resources; people, equipment and rooms
                - contingency plans and back up
                - thought for the customer (pupil/group/parent)
                - involvement, encouragement of ideas, development
                - decision making

Execution: where the planned lesson is put into operation
                - ability to reassess and be flexible
                - class based factors (motivation, support, involvement)
                - communication skills
                - decision taking
                - consideration for the pupil/group
                - general control and discipline

Of course, such a model is extremely general and we would not suggest rigidly applying it to every piece of lesson preparation! However, it remains a good general guide.

It is interesting to note that the final point in the execution of the task is control and discipline. Quite often you will find that when your self and work preparation is good, then control becomes a natural part of the lesson. Part of this self preparation concerns self projection. This involves the presentation of yourself as a concerned, caring, balanced individual. We will return to this later. Let us first concentrate on the quality of your preparation. It is clearly impossible to take into account all the factors mentioned in the list each time you prepare a lesson – this would be impractical in a busy average week with a full timetable. However, the efficiency which develops with experience will enable you to maximise your effect with an economy of effort – it will become easier in your first year of teaching. In conversation with other colleagues you may hear of the term 'door handle' teaching. This is where a teacher decides upon the work for the lesson as he turns the door handle into the classroom. This is something all experienced teachers have succumbed to occasionally but if it becomes a habit it will create fraught teaching situations and

Figure 1.

ACTION CHECKLIST			
Key Actions	Task	Class	Individual
Define objectives	Identify task(s) and constraints Establish	Involve all members of class Share commitment	Clarify objectives Gain acceptance
Organise	Check resources Make decisions Set standards	Consult Encourage ideas and actions Develop suggestions	Assess skills Set targets Assign roles Delegate
Communicate	Brief the class Check understanding	Answer questions Obtain feedback	Listen Encourage
Control	Report progress Maintain standards Discipline	Co-ordinate Resolve conflict	Advise Assist/reassure Recognise effort Counsel
Evaluate	Summarise progress Review objectives Replan if necessary	Recognise success Learn from failure	Assess performance Appraise Guide and train

an environment conducive to disorder. It is also lazy and unprofessional, whilst contravening the contract under which teachers are employed following the 1989 Education Act. It cannot be stressed too highly that adequate preparation will minimise the risk of disruption.

At this point it is worth emphasising that your class is made up of individuals with different needs. To regard a class as an identity rather than as a collection of individuals is dangerous and, with an all-ability teaching group, your preparation is going to have to show that.

There are five key stages in a teacher's preparation and execution of a lesson; define objectives, organise, communicate, control and evaluate. In the table (Figure 1) observe how these actions break down into a planned strategy for a programme of work. Notice how both group and individual needs are catered for.

This checklist is neither prescriptive nor exhaustive. It is designed to make you aware of the complex and finely tuned work you perform. Clearly every lesson cannot be planned with such detail. You will find, however, as you become involved in this 'awareness' approach that many of the items listed are considered and used without conscious referral to them. Having prepared the work and the majority of the resources of the lesson, what about yourself? *You* are the most important resource. Your knowledge and the way in which you communicate it is the key feature in the learning process for those in your care.

You will continually seek to be aware of your pupils as individuals and an awareness of the individual members of your group is essential. Your knowledge of key personalities will help you prepare for and prevent any challenge to your authority. You are a skilled practitioner. You have many techniques at your disposal with which to offer care and control. The young people in your class will *expect* control. Give it to them in the first instance by sound work and self-preparation and you will receive an appropriate response from them.

The effect of teacher personality

In the process of your delivery your personality will either help or hinder you. There is a tendency for young people to fix their attention not on the subject matter of the lesson but on the teacher who delivers it. All subjects can be potentially interesting: it is sometimes the teacher or other factors which prevent pupils becoming motivated by the material. In your avoidance of unwanted behaviour there is a need to remember factors such as your own awareness, your attitude to the class, your ability to be creative and your own personality. In the experience of the authors, young people feel more secure when boundaries are drawn up by the teacher and adhered to; they also thrive on friendships, understanding, acceptance and honesty. As Carl Rogers (1983) states, 'The three most vital characteristics of an effective worker with people whether in one-to-one or group situations are:

- Genuineness – be open and believable.
- Warm acceptance – listen and show that you care.
- Empathetic understanding – hear the feelings behind the words.

Without these three characteristics, all the skills and techniques will be to no avail.'

Chapter Eight offers a simple checklist procedure, but it may be useful to summarise some basic guidelines which will help you to create a climate of trust and cooperation in which anti-social behaviour will find it difficult to flourish.

DO
(1) Be prepared and organised.
(2) Have contingency plans available.
(3) Have enough work available.
(4) Create your own thinking space.
(5) Make realistic expectations.
(6) Be consistent.
(7) Take a sensible balanced approach.
(8) Admit you are human and can be wrong.
(9) Present yourself respectably.
(10) Be a caring, professional person.
(11) Maintain your position firmly with dignity and composure.
(12) Explain how views differ and why.

DO NOT
(1) Increase conflict by unnecessary confrontation.
(2) Humiliate pupils.
(3) Indicate that you will consider the matter.
(4) Always accede to demands or requests too soon. This will create 'thinking space'.
(5) Always trust pupils implicitly; instead, let them know that they are likely to be the subjects of random checks.
(6) Leave a class unattended.

116

(7) Allow yourself to be drawn into disagreement when you do not wish it.
(8) Threaten/promise knowing that you cannot deliver.
(9) Offer to do too much too soon.
(10) Bully or be sarcastic.

Crisis intervention

Sound preparation and awareness will help prevent much unwanted behaviour but there will always be the occasion when conflict arises and some form of intervention is necessary. Why should you do anything at all? There are three main reasons:

● The behaviour presumed to be 'maladaptive' occurs at sufficient strength (both in frequency and duration) as to cause concern.
● The behaviour if continued will harm the pupil or his immediate environment.
● The behaviour would be likely to impede the learning process and healthy development.

These occasions are never pleasant and can arrive spontaneously or develop slowly and obviously. The eventual outburst in either case can erupt with great speed, often before the misbehaver is aware of it herself. What do you do, and how do you retrieve the situation in such a way as to enable the child to back down and the status quo to be resumed?

Your action

You need to move decisively and carefully. Your first priority is safety of other pupils, those involved in the conflict and you. You are going to need to reduce conflict and/or minimise damage whilst preventing the incident from escalating out of proportion. Again, you must develop the skill of defusing or 'removing the heat' from the situation. This is achieved by removing the source of conflict.

Be aware when putting someone out of the room, of the implications of that action. For example, is the behaviour going to continue outside? Could there be damage to others or nearby property? Even though a pupil is outside your room waiting by the door, that person remains your responsibility. Can you observe them adequately by this action? It may be better to control within the classroom; to tell the rest of the class to get on with work set and then give the pupil(s) specific attention on site. Other methods can be employed such as:

- Change the seating positions.
- Change work set.
- Send a message via a trusted pupil to a more senior colleague.
- Ignore the provocation and continue teaching.
- Control the situation by polite, firm but non-demeaning statements.

There are other methods available. These, as with any approach, will only be effective when it is relevant and suitable to the occasion. The timing and selection of the most appropriate response will become easier as your experience grows. In some cases your common sense will dictate your actions. However, it will always be possible to make mistakes. We all have done and will continue to do so at times. Most important is the ability to act appropriately in the majority of situations. As before there are some dos and don'ts:

DO
(1) Minimise damage.
(2) Reduce conflict escalation.
(3) Isolate if necessary for 'cooling off'.
(4) Remain calm.
(5) Be professional.
(6) Be positive.
(7) Be objective.

DO NOT
(1) Use sarcasm/innuendo.
(2) Belittle or bully.
(3) Tell off in group situations.
(4) Refer to senior staff too soon.
(5) Label.
(6) Physically or verbally abuse.

The 'don'ts' are especially important. Failure to restrict these practices leads to unfair treatment and the inhibition of any repair of the damage between teacher and pupil. This leads us to a further consideration.

Once you have intervened in the crisis, the relationship between you and those involved must be returned to a stable condition as soon as possible. For both sides, learning from the experience may be very difficult: impressions of the sequence of events may be different; there may be bitterness; there is always a need to maintain self respect. Not all crisis interventions result in a poor relationship between pupil and teacher but unfair and misdirected tensions have a tendency to spill over and affect others. On these occasions it may be useful to for teacher and pupil, separately or together, to have a framework for guidance:

- Explain to themselves and others how they felt before, during and after the event.
- Identify where perceptions of what happened coincide and vary.
- Understand how their feelings may have shaped their version of events.

It is clear that to come to terms with any of the above, issues of trust, confidentiality and expectation need careful consideration. Let us examine these more closely.

Trust – Going back over painful scenes, trying to be honest and receptive is not easy. For teachers and pupils there needs to be mutual trust.

Confidentiality – Is important. It encourages trust. Records of personal details and judgements may be made: will they be destroyed after use?

Expectation – None of these methods will ensure that confrontation leads to better understanding. Both sides need realistic expectations. The earlier drawing up of clear parameters of behaviour by you as the teacher will lead to clearer expectations of what is and isn't possible.

It is immediately apparent that both teacher and pupil will undergo the same processes. Pupils need to see teachers as examples of that which schools want them to become. You cannot set an example of balanced adult behaviour by screaming at a pupil and looking at his/her behaviour only through your eyes.

To help be objective in this emotionally charged atmosphere, a simple incident recording form may be used which teacher and pupil can use as a starting point for negotiation after confrontation. The form need only record basic information such as:

(1) Time of incident.
(2) Place.
(3) What I was doing before the incident?
(4) How I was feeling before the incident?
(5) What I think sparked off the incident.

(6) Describe what happened as you remember it.
(7) Give as much detail as you can, including, if it is important, what other pupils said or did during the incident.

The following points give guidelines for beginning negotiations:

- the meeting needs to take place as soon as possible after the event.
- both need to agree to spend, say, ten minutes filling in the form, prior to the meeting.
- completed forms can be exchanged or read out section by section.
- feelings expressed in sections 3 and 4 need to be accepted by both parties before moving on.
- all discrepancies need noting before they are challenged.
- both parties need to make 'I' statements instead of 'you' statements.
- where there is no agreement, acknowledgement must be made.
- if an observer/arbitrator is used, both parties need to trust and respect them.

For youngsters with poor writing skills a taped account could be used. The format is not as important as the process of calmly going through the issues raised. This can end in stalemate. More often than not it provides a platform for discussion away from the heat of the moment.

Conflict situations and crisis interventions need to be learning situations for both you, the teacher, and the pupil. The end result of conflict must be some kind of resolution; progress should be made towards overcoming the disagreement with an appropriate saving of 'face' and maintenance of self respect by both parties.

Long term unwanted behaviour

Crisis intervention is instant, with short term answers to immediate problems. You will encounter some children whose needs are long term, even beyond the scope of the school experience. Such long term behaviour issues need careful treatment and often will need the help of senior staff member and/or outside agencies. This latter resource has been detailed in an earlier chapter; a summary of factors in such referrals occurs below.

The process needs to be:

● positive, dynamic and current
● fair and appropriate
● focussed and standardised.

Any such mechanism used needs to consider that:

- difficult behaviours will not be eliminated overnight.
- steady step by step progress is needed towards a stable level of acceptable behaviour.
- teachers and school are effective agents for socialisation by providing systematic learning experiences.

Such considerations make it possible for the behaviourist approach to be appropriate in dealing with long term behaviour issues. This formal behaviour management programme has the following components which make it an effective method of controlling and subsequently changing behaviour.

(1) Identify the problem.
(2) Define/elaborate the definition of the problem.
(3) Assess the baseline upon which to work and select priorities.
(4) Identify reinforcer and contingency factors. Generate solutions and plan strategies.
(5) Implement the programme.
(6) Observe and evaluate effects of programme.
(7) Modify programme according to (6).
(8) Fade out programme.

In such a programme there is a continuous emphasis on planning and making it meet the needs of the individual. Some children become reliant upon such a structure. Consequently, there is a distinct 'weaning off' component to enable the individual to behave in a 'normal' way in an everyday environment.

These unwanted long term behaviours are likely to impinge upon your teaching programmes. With such pupils you will benefit from advice and help from more experienced colleagues. Do not be afraid to ask for help. All experienced teachers have a memory bank of actions and responses from which they will be only too willing to assist. That you are able to turn to such colleagues is in itself testimony to the fact that a growth in experience will gradually make your task easier. Developing strategies for dealing with deviant behaviour is a learning process undergone by all teachers throughout their careers.

All unwanted behaviour will test you. It has tested all of us and you will be no exception. The secret lies in your adjustment and flexibility in handling what happens in front of you. Your preparation, your professionalism, your determination to succeed in teaching and the advice and support of colleagues will all combine in equipping you to manage your classroom in an efficient, caring and educative way.

CHAPTER 8

Back to Basic Principles

Although it is difficult to quantify the infinite variety of situations which can occur in schools, it is possible to identify *typical* incidents and suggest an appropriate response. An experienced teacher will absorb unconsciously from colleagues (who may be good or bad role models!) a range of responses over a period of years. This, coupled with experience gained from coping with problems oneself, is the usual source of professional expertise.

In this chapter we have assembled a range of hints and tips which is designed to be referred to as the situation demands, or prior to taking up a teaching post. The sections of the chapter are: Before You Start, Getting Started, Dealing with Problems, Rounding Off the Lesson. Each section follows a Dos and Don'ts format.

Before you start

DO

Assume nothing! Keep an open mind. A first year class is just as likely to lack pens or equipment as a fifth year class. Be initially sparing with your trust.

Count equipment – at the beginning of the lesson and after handing in at the end.

Be in the classroom before your pupils arrive.

Line the pupils up quietly outside the classroom before entering especially for the first few lessons.

Bring a box of pens, rulers, rubbers and other equipment to the lesson to allow for loss and failure of pupils to bring their own.

Make sure that the lesson is not comprised of only one activity. Some pupils cannot concentrate for long periods. Have some activities in reserve. Have contingency plans if the first strategy fails.

122

Make sure that videos and other equipment work prior to the children being in the room for the lesson.

Give advance warning to your class that you require a particular piece of equipment for a given lesson. Do not rely on a message via colleagues – they may forget!

Seat your pupils in an appropriate manner to your lesson, i.e. in groups for discussion, or facing the front for more formal teaching.

Use a teaching style (experiential/didactic) as appropriate to the lesson material and context. All have their place.

DON'T

Take your own problems to the classroom. Leave them at home, in the car or in the staffroom.

Allow pupils to sit with their backs to you even in rooms with chairs grouped around tables. The simplest solution is to move yourself to a suitable position in the room.

Court popularity. Pupils will like you if you treat them fairly and consistently. They are quick to spot weakness.

Be tempted to lend money/personal possessions to pupils. At all costs avoid borrowing money.

Be influenced by the staffroom cynic. Every school has at least one and those cynical remarks are often part of harmless staffroom banter. Avoid classifying colleagues.

Be aggressive with pupils for image making purposes but it is wise to be firm initially thereby allowing for later relaxation.

Getting started

DO

Settle the class before starting. Avoid talking over noise. Wait calmly and expectantly by looking at each pupil in turn. Silence will descend!

Explain what you are setting out to achieve in that lesson and why you are asking pupils to do a particular piece of work.

Respect the dignity of your pupils and their views.

Use eye contact with your pupils when you are speaking to them. They soon understand that this means that you are both relaxed and confident. Smile!

Move around the room even if reading to your pupils. Sometimes teach from the middle or the back of the class. It helps to maintain interest and stop them becoming complacent. Adopt a relaxed stance and select the best vantage points.

Vary your voice in the way you might in conversation.

Be prepared to see the funny side of situations and allow yourself to relax and laugh with your class.

Admit you are human and can be wrong.

Learn names as quickly as possible. The ability to refer to people personally and directly enhances relationships and enables you to identify the source of your concerns individually.

DON'T

Panic if someone is upsetting your lesson. Keep calm and try to be objective. Do not resort to threats or tactics which you know will not work or which you will be unable to carry out.

Give detentions without 24 hours notice to parents. This is a courtesy.

Aim for impossible standards. Assess pupils' needs and abilities, then build gradually.

Criticise too often. Try to find something to praise.

Falsely praise. Pupils are much more perceptive than you think.

Dealing with problems

DO

Remain calm. Create your own thinking space. Your first aim is to take the heat out of the situation.

Check unwanted behaviours early. They will not go away if you don't.

Be consistent in applying reprimands, punishments and rewards.

Issue notes to any pupil leaving your room explaining destination and time of departure from lesson.

Move pupils if talking or misbehaving. Isolate trouble makers.

DON'T

Hoist pupils up the punishment tariff by over reaction or unnecessary escalation of the problem.

Be tempted to send a pupil out of the room to a senior member of staff unless the incident is really serious. Try to deal with the problem yourself within the classroom, asking later for advice from more experienced colleagues. Ask someone to come into your lesson only as a last resort and then to help *you* to deal with the situation, rather than take it away.

Carry on talking if you detect someone else talking. Stop and calmly look at the individual concerned who will then look uneasy and stop. Then continue yourself.

Be personal when dealing out admonishments. Punish the offence, not the person.

Over-react to an explosion of temper, defiance, rudeness or other outburst. Remember that your first aim is to lower the temperature and avoid outright confrontation. (This does not however, mean that you ignore or fail to deal with a situation in order to avoid it). Also the rest of the class need to be kept working, therefore avoid providing them with an entertaining spectacle. Keep your voice reasonable and low and ask the pupil to go out of the room and speak to him/her there. Avoid humiliating a pupil in front of class. This could lead to major confrontation. In many cases the pupil will go back into class quietly and continue with work.

Be embarrassed (if you can) when pupils make a personal observation or remark about you. Calmly fend off questions about your private life and volunteer only such information that you don't mind being common currency around school. If some aspect of your dress requires adjusting, adjust it calmly retaining your dignity with humour. Do not allow your pupils to think you are embarrassed, even if you are.

Rounding off the lesson

DO

Have a routine with finishing. Collecting in equipment helps. Ask a trusted pupil to help. They will soon get used to your routine and will feel safe within the structure you create.

Settle the class at the end making them sit quietly before asking them to pick up any litter, etc. Then ask them to stand and put their chairs under the tables, or as appropriate. Structure of this type helps the routines of calmness.

Clean the chalkboard completely if you have used it. Leave it for the next teacher in the condition you would like to find it.

Maintain your idealism and optimism even if things have not gone totally to plan. There is always tomorrow.

DON'T

Allow pupils to leave the room unless you are happy with the state of it. Never allow them to run out. Dismiss them, if necessary, row by row.

CHAPTER 9

And So to Monday . . .

Your first day of 'real' teaching approaches – all your training, school practice and study has led you to this point. You are confident but a little nervous; although you are certain that you will make a long term success of your appointment, how will you be able to measure how well you are progressing?

For a variety of reasons, the classroom management skills of any teacher are subject to a most subjective wide-spread scrutiny. Every adult in this country has been taught in a classroom. He or she will have related to different learning experiences in different ways and will, therefore, have a definite opinion on what is a 'good classroom teacher'.

From your first Monday morning and from that first lesson onwards you will be subjected to the closest scrutiny by the most demanding of consumers – the pupils and, by implication, their parents. From the first moment they will be forming a view of your effectiveness. These first impressions will influence their attitude towards you, your teaching style and the classroom environment in the long term.

As we have maintained throughout the book, there is a need to develop preventative approaches in dealing with crisis management. Our aim has been to raise your awareness of this fact by examination of the main causal factors.

The complexity of your role as a classroom teacher is obvious and the effective learning environment you wish to create will be affected by your understanding of its importance. Chief elements in this complex role are the organisational, administrative and inter-personal skills. At different times each may play a more dominant role than others but competence and confidence in all three areas provide the key to the preventative approach. In the experience of the authors the effectiveness of the teacher as a classroom manager is measured by the ability to use skill, judgement and knowledge in these three areas.

For the inexperienced teacher such judgement and knowledge will come with time and a willingness to learn from experience. In the short term, (before that first Monday) make sure that you take the following steps:

(1) Plan an outline of the term's work for each group you are to take and in detail the first week's lessons. Do not worry if you have to change or modify the lessons after meeting your groups. Get to know and understand the work schemes and/or syllabus requirements as well as the room(s) in which you will work. You will normally spend at least a day in the school prior to taking up your post, whilst it is possible to arrange a visit during the school holidays.

(2) Organise other resources in preparation for the practicalities of the first few lessons; pens, pencils, worksheets, charts, audio-visual aids and so on.

(3) Be aware of the reward systems and sanctions which you can impose and of any other aspect of the school's disciplinary code of which you should have knowledge. In addition, find out the routes of positive feedback available to you and which you might successfully employ in creating the environment which you desire.

(4) Make it your business to know the nature of the resources available outside the classroom to help you to maintain a preventative approach.

(5) If possible, organise your timetable for work preparation, taking books in to mark and other administrative necessities, in advance. Good time management is the key to much of what brings confident, clear-sighted, unruffled teaching. If it is not possible to do this in advance, work out a system as soon as you are able. It is vital.

Following these steps will enable you to make a start, confident that you have done everything possible to ensure a smooth start to your career. From such a start it will be easier to deal with the minor problems which occur in the classroom. These happen to everybody!

Having prepared well in advance, how do you judge success? Judging successful teaching as an aspect of teacher appraisal has been, as you will be aware, a contentious issue. Whatever the merits, or otherwise of appraisal, it is natural to wish to know how one is performing and to look for a yardstick with which to compare oneself.

In your first year of teaching you will of course undergo appraisal. It is usual for probationary teachers to be attached to a senior member of staff who will organise regular seminars or meetings, be available for advice and oversee your progress. In addition your Head of Department will observe some of your lessons and will be available to offer you constructive advice. L.E.A. Advisers or Inspectors will also have such a role. These personnel all contribute towards the writing of probationary reports, which are required termly.

In these reports the positive aspects of your work will be commented upon, whilst any noted weaknesses will be coupled with suggested methods for effecting an improvement. It is not unusual for teachers to be left to their own devices and little effective feedback is received. It must be stressed that this is not always the case and many departments are extremely supportive of colleagues within them. However, unless a model of appraisal is in use in your school, it is likely that the formal period of your teacher development will cease at the end of your probationary year.

In addition to this process you will find it useful to set your own targets by which to judge yourself. The range of possible targets is immense and may well vary from one class to the next. Examples of areas to consider could be as follows:

- Pupils always enter the classroom in a sensible manner, prepare their desks and resources quickly and wait quietly for the lesson to start. In this case your aim has been to ensure that pupils *are aware* of your view of how the lesson should begin, have accepted your parameters of attitudes and behaviour in this situation and that your organisation skills at the start of the lesson are effective. If this is happening then success has been achieved. If there are difficulties, the opportunity is presented to assess and to rectify the cause.

- You wish to ensure that all homework is done satisfactorily by all pupils. This may happen automatically, but it might be necessary to call on your administrative and interpersonal skills to coax some pupils to reach your required standard. It may also need input from someone in a more senior position in the school. When considering your success, it will be necessry to examine how you handled the situation, what elements you could or could not control, whether you used sanctions carefully, whether you were demanding too much of some or not enough of others. Through such reflection you may be able to redefine your targets for future use.

● Your relationships with pupils will be an area in which you wish to find success. This is not to imply that you would wish to court popularity but that you want to set up an effective, co-operative working environment with which you feel happy, when dealing with both the individual and the class. Again, you need to define 'effectiveness' in terms of the class or individual – you will not have the same working relationships with two different classes automatically and so, therefore, your target for success will need to be flexible. If you fail to reach your target it will then be necessary to reflect, analyse and redefine your aims once more.

There are many other possible examples. You may wish to consider relationships with parents, colleagues, the success or otherwise of your pupils reaching National Curriculum attainment targets, or, say, internal exams. With continually assessed G.C.S.E. courses it will be possible to monitor the coursework of your pupils which will show some element of success but for the classroom teacher, the day to day aspects of the class teacher role may yield only a feeling of routine and a 'production line' mentality. Regular appraisal of one's own performance coupled with a willingness to adopt new or different attitudes can provide the freshness and interest which all teachers need to keep if they are to maintain their enthusiasm and, consequently that of their pupils.

Occasionally a pupil will tell you that a lesson was good or interesting, or, if he or she is really brave, might comment positively on your performance. Such instances are scarce, however, and the reasons for them may not always be those which you consider to be important. Thus, your own goals and standards should, in most cases, provide the base from which you work.

The complexity of the teacher's role is clear; the background of skills, aptitudes and knowledge which are required before entering the classroom and which can be developed with experience in order to become increasingly effective, are vital.

As a result of these factors, teaching is undoubtedly a demanding, sometimes frustrating, always varied but generally rewarding career. It is necessary to bear in mind your ideals, your goals, and to work towards them optimistically and with flexibility. The background we have supplied is intended to provide a basis from which to work towards the achievement of success. The practical nature of the occupation means that those of us who have worked in the profession for some years are likely to feel a greater sense of security and confidence in the classroom. This is the value of experience, common to any occupation, which you will acquire in time. It is the earnest hope of the authors of this book that we have been able to share with you some of that experience so that, on that first Monday, or indeed any day, you will feel some measure of confidence when confronted with that first effervescent group of young people.

Above all, teaching is never dull, never routine and there is always something new to learn. Accept this, and be prepared to build on the knowledge which you already have and you will find no more rewarding occupation.

Good luck!

Bibliography

Bald, J. (1982) 'Children in Care'. *Concern*. Cited by Sonia Jackson, see reference

Chisholm, B. *et al*. (1984) *Preventative Approach to Disruption. Developing Teaching Skills*. London: Croom Helm

Coulby, D. and Harper, T. (1985) *Preventing Classroom Disruption. Policy, Practice and Evaluation in Urban Schools*. London: Croom Helm

Emmerson, C. and Goddard, L. (1989) *All About the National Curriculum*. Oxford and London: Heinemann Educational

Galloway, D. and Goodwin, C. (1979) *Educating Slow Learning and Maladjusted Children: Integration or Segregation?* London: Longman

Hazel, N. (1981) *A Bridge to Independence: The Kent Family Placement Project*. Oxford: Basil Blackwell

Jackson, Sonia (1987) *The Education of Children in Care*. Bristol: University of Bristol

Macbeth, A. (1989) *Involving Parents*. Oxford and London: Heinemann Educational

Marland, M. (1986) *School Management Skills*. Oxford and London: Heinemann Educational

National Association for Young People in Care (1883) Evidence to the House of Commons Social Services Committee's Enquiry into Children in Care. NAYPIC: Bradford

Rogers, C. (1983) *Freedom to Learn in the Eighties*. USA: Merrill

Rutter, M. *et al*. (1979) *Fifteen Thousand Hours*. London: Open Books

Topping, K. (1983) *Educational Systems for Disruptive Adolescents*. Beckenham, Kent: Croom Helm

Warnock, M. (1978) *Special Needs in Education* (The Warnock Report). London: HMSO

Index

ABC of behavioural analysis 93,
   94, 103, 107, 109–110
Acceptance 115
achievement 63, 71
Administrative necessities 77
Agencies, outside 83
All ability 18, 42
Antecedents 107
Area Health Authority 91
Area Education Officer 88
assessment 59–60
Assessment, multi-professional 89
Attendance checks 76
awareness 114, 115

background, pupils' 20–21
banding 17
behavioural analysis 103, 105–107
behaviourism 103
boundary checking 106

careers service 91
challenging behaviour 35
child response resource team 91
Colleges, City Technology (C.T.C.)
   2–3
composition of catchment 2
comments, positive 77, 78
concentration, pupils' 38–39
confidentiality 118
conflict 116
constraints 16
C.P.V.E. 40

crisis intervention 103, 116–119
curriculum 11, 14, 32–34
curriculum, pattern and effect of
   11, 14

departmental strengths 13
difficulties, discussion of 79
dignity 122
disaffection 35
discussion work 58–59
disruption 105–106
disturbed behaviour, categories of
   106
duration 106

Education Act, 1944 52
Education Department 88, 89
Educational Psychologist 89
Education Reform Act 1988 33
Education Welfare Officer 85
embarrassment 124
empathetic understanding 115
environment (classroom) 4–9
equipment 4
evaluation of lessons 44
exam performance 12–13
expectation 118

Frequency 106

G.C.S.E. 19, 20, 21, 51, 128

Home Tuition Service 89

134